Faith of our Fathers

Faith of our Fathers

Reflections on Catholic Tradition

EAMON DUFFY

continuum

LONDON • NEW YORK

Published in Association with
Priests and People

CONTINUUM
The Tower Building, 11 York Road, London SE1 7NX
15 East 26th Street, New York NY 10010

www.continuumbooks.com

First published 2004

British Library Cataloguing-in-Publication Data
A catalogue record for this book is available from the British Library.

ISBN: 0-8264-7479-9

Typeset by Kenneth Burnley, Wirral, Cheshire
Printed and bound in Great Britain by MPG Books Ltd, Bodmin, Cornwall

Contents

Preface

Roman Catholics have always attributed a special value to their Church's past, for they believe that the saving truth of God is encountered not merely in the pages of the Bible, but in the proclamation, worship and shared experience of the Christian community – that complex expression of lived faith which we call the tradition. Yet in the latter twentieth century the Catholic Church underwent a dramatic and, to many, disturbing transformation, which seemed to open up a deep gulf between modern believers and their past. Anyone raised a Catholic before 1965 was formed in a Church which understood and presented itself as essentially timeless, its worship and its law enshrined (or, from another perspective, entombed) in the immemorial splendours of the Latin language, its authority structures dominated by its clergy, its principal teachings infallible and therefore irreformable. Roman Catholics had little contact with Christians from other traditions, and were indeed forbidden to worship or even to recite the Lord's Prayer in common with them. A 'fortress mentality' prevailed, Church against world, which in Britain and in America was underpinned by the ethnic and social history of Catholics, many of whom were first-, second- or third-generation descendants of economic migrants, not always entirely at ease in the society around them.

The reforms initiated by the Second Vatican Council, which met from 1962 to 1965, profoundly changed the experience of Catholics at every level. The monolith seemed to crumble, immobility gave way to flux. In the wake of the Council, worship was simplified and translated into the vernacular, and almost overnight the Latin liturgy, with its millennia-long repertoire of sacred music, became an exotic rarity: plainchant and renaissance polyphony were replaced by folk hymns accompanied by guitar and electronic keyboard. Catholic churches were 'reordered' to allow the clergy to face the people across the altar, and much of their traditional liturgical furniture and imagery was discarded as redundant. These ritual and organizational changes reflected profound theological reorientation as the older certainties of the seminary textbooks were challenged and replaced by theologies which emphasized engagement with social issues and openness to other Christians. Catholics were now encouraged to throw themselves into ecumenical activity, and structures were democratized to give lay people greater scope for involvement.

The religious ferment which began in the mid-1960s was part of a much wider social and cultural unsettlement. The sexual revolution which began then found its more decorous counterpart in the Roman Catholic debate over artificial methods of birth control, and the rethinking of authority and hierarchy with which Catholics were wrestling was inevitably influenced by the widespread suspicion of power and the structures of power which were the special mark of the 1960s and 1970s. It was an exhilarating time, filled with the sense of momentous and life-giving transformations, the bursting of constraints and the opening of new possibilities. For many who lived through them, myself included, these were unforgettable and formative years. But it was also a time of naïve and sometimes philistine incomprehension of the past which had formed us, in which much that was precious was disparaged or discarded. In this atmosphere, to suggest that an idea or an institution was old-fashioned was often enough to discredit it. 'Pre-Conciliar' became a term of abuse or dismissal. It is now possible to see just how wholesale and indiscriminate this communal repudiation of the past was, and in a Church which claims to set a high theological value on tradition and continuity, this is a mystery which needs explanation.

It is a mystery because by and large in the past Catholic theologians advocating change, even radical change, have been as anxious to invoke the notion of tradition as those seeking to maintain the *status quo*. At the heart of the 'New Theology' of De Lubac, Congar and the other theological midwives of the Council, was a passionate call to *rediscover* the tradition. They set about freeing the Church from the narrow straitjacket of a debased nineteenth-century neo-scholasticism by opening up the riches of the deep tradition of the Church, in the scriptures, the liturgy, the Fathers. For them the past was not a sterile cul-de-sac to be escaped from, but an inexhaustible well of Christian experience and wisdom, which liberated theology and the Christian imagination by demonstrating how diverse, subtle, endlessly inventive the Church has been, and is called to be, in her journey through time.

Within Ultramontane Catholicism, however, the notion of tradition had been in danger of narrowing to mean little more than the current Roman theology. Pio Nono's notorious 1870 aphorism '*I am* the tradition', was a telling reflection of the day-to-day reality of an increasingly powerful central authority, which strangled Catholic theology (and episcopal teaching) for a century. Most of the citations in the (rejected) draft declaration of faith drawn up for the Second Vatican Council by the Holy Office under Cardinal Ottaviani, for example, were from the writings and speeches of Pius XII and his immediate predecessors: no church document earlier than the Council of Trent was cited, and there were no quotations from scripture. Tradition had shrunk from being a cathedral of the Spirit to a storeroom in the cellars of the Holy Office.

The Conciliar reforms did a great deal to correct this sterile and authoritarian notion of tradition, to recover a sense of the variety and richness of the Christian past as a resource for the Christian present. But whatever the roots of reform, much of the practical liturgical, theological and catechetical reform carried out since the Second Vatican Council was informed by a search for immediacy or authenticity of experience, rather than attentive encounter with the diversity, depth and wisdom of the tradition. In place of a philistine authoritarianism, cut off from the riches and complexity of the Christian past by a mindset described as 'non-historical orthodoxy', we have tended to substitute a non-historical liberalism, which has even less to offer. *I fear - Yes*

Reaction was inevitable, and drew strength from the fact that the years immediately before the Council proved to have been the high-watermark of institutional Roman Catholicism in Britain and North America. In the wake of the Council, thousands and priests and religious abandoned their vocations to marry, clerical recruitment plummeted, and Catholic practice eroded. Unsurprisingly, the blame for this institutional erosion was often laid at the door of post-Conciliar change. Accordingly, over the last 20 years there has been a growing call for 'restoration', endorsed at the highest levels of the Church, and manifesting itself in a revived clericalism and a strong-arm exercise of ecclesiastical authority which many find deeply alienating. 'Tradition' has become a fraught and difficult term, invoked by self-styled 'traditionalists', to call a halt to change and herald a return to the forms and mindset of the recent past, rather than as a resource for change.

The essays in this book were written out of a quite contrary conviction, that an understanding of the richness of the Church's past is a liberation, not a straitjacket. The tradition offers us a point of vantage from which to criticize the present, certainly, but it is also a source of confidence in launching into the uncharted future. Cardinal Newman once famously declared that 'in another world it may be otherwise, but here below to live is to change, and to be perfect is to have changed often'. The Church's past, in all its complexity and contradictoriness, is abundant evidence that change, not stasis, is the sign of life.

These essays are all in origin occasional pieces, most of them written for the journal *Priests and People*. They make no claim to comprehensive coverage of the Catholic faith, but I hope that they do offer a consistent and useful perspective on many of the central concerns of Catholic Christianity at the start of the third millennium. Fr David Saunders, OP, editor of *Priests and People*, commissioned most of the pieces, and first suggested that they would make a coherent and worthwhile book. I dedicate that book to him, and to the memory of his Dominican colleague Herbert McCabe, from whose friendship and example I learned something of the roller-coaster exhilaration of faith seeking understanding.

EAMON DUFFY
Epiphany, 2004

1

Prologue:
When Belief Fails

The following is an abbreviated extract from an address entitled 'When belief fails', originally delivered in Great St Mary's Church as part of a Cambridge University Mission, and first published in New Black-friars *in May 1985.*

I find myself a beachcomber along the edges of the sea of faith. I am to speak of unbelief, to try to pick from the flotsam and jetsam of my own experience some reflections on doubts about the existence of God and the worth of religion. And I want to register at the beginning my own scepticism about the notion that it is somehow *harder* for modern people to believe because we *know* more, *understand* more, about the world than people in the past. Belief in God, in the God of Abraham and Isaac and Jacob, the God who acted in Jesus, who was before the worlds and will survive them, the God from whom we are born and into whom we will die: belief in that God is not now and never has been a matter of a collection of opinions and ideas about how the world started or how it works; it is not rooted in bad physics. The saints and theologians and simple believers of the past cannot be dismissed as a bunch of flat-earthers, whose God is some sort of discredited spiritual technology. Belief in God is now what it has always been, a matter of trust and reliance in the hopefulness and goodness of reality, and our place in it. Knowledge as such hardly affects it, and cannot in itself hinder or help it. Ask yourself; who will find it harder to believe in a loving and caring creator – a secure Western scientist in search of explanations in a well-funded laboratory, or a peasant woman in Ethiopia whose children have starved to death before her eyes? The things which make belief in God difficult are not the inventions of our age, but the perennial tragedy and brokenness of human existence.

So I am unimpressed by the suggestion that the undoubted marginalizing of religion in our society has much, or anything, to do with knowledge or intellectual advance. I think the explanation lies elsewhere. Since the onset of the Enlightenment, for at least 300 years, we in the West have been systematically constructing a world in which men and women are dehumanized, pushed into anonymous multitudes, as 'hands' in the production of commodities, or as 'consumers' in an economy dominated not by human needs, but by market forces. And within these collectivities they have been isolated, peddled an understanding of identity which is defined by separation from others, peddled an understanding of freedom as unfettered individualism. Our closest bonds are vested interest, or solidarity for the purposes of waging war. We strip our common discourse of all but utilitarian words and notions, and then greet the disappearance of non-utilitarian concerns beliefs as surprising and somehow a measure of progress. We put out our eyes, and then insist that the sun is a fiction of the poets.

But humanity is not by its nature the inhabitant of what D. H. Lawrence called the 'dry sterile little world the abstract mind inhabits'. The matter is essentially a simple one. Empty society of the experience of shared value and commitment, exclude wonder and reverence as legitimate human responses to the world, isolate men and women within the trap of their own limited and limiting goals, and they will cease to speak of God. They will have forgotten his name, because they will not know their own.

> It was there that they asked us,
> Our captors, for songs,
> Our oppressors, for joy.

> Sing to us, they said, one of Sion's songs.
> O how could we sing
> The song of the Lord
> On alien soil? (Psalm 136)

If there is any truth at all that we live in an age of doubt, it lies not in the advance of knowledge, but in the impoverishment of our collective perceptions, in the emptying of our language and our society of anything but number and calculation. The poet William Blake saw it coming and denounced it, at the beginning of the modern era:

> What, it will be questioned, when the sun rises, do you not see a round disc of fire somewhat like a guinea?
> O no, I see an innumerable company of the heavenly host crying HOLY HOLY HOLY is the Lord God Almighty.

But of course lack of belief cannot just be explained away by social conditioning, any more than belief can. Doubt, the fear that the world has no direction, that all humankind's aspirations are trivialized by death, the death of the individual or the generation or – a new possibility in our time – the species, the conviction that our goodness passes away and our evil can never be undone; these things touch all of us. If we are to be believers, it cannot be by pretending that no one has these feelings, or that they are not formidable and persuasive. It cannot be by pretending that we do not feel them ourselves.

I have no claim to expertise in these matters, and I have no illusion that my experience or perception of things has any sort of exemplary status. But in thinking about the failure of belief, I thought that the best thing I could do was to describe my own failure of belief. Not the repeated infidelities, the hundred failures of commitment and conviction that seem to make the substance of my life as a Christian; but one particular period in my life when, quite simply, I became certain that there was no God, and that Christianity was an illusion.

I had my basic religious education from Irish religious

brothers, in the bad old days before the Second Vatican Council. It was a tough training, involving total saturation in Catholic subculture, 'God is Love' thumped into you with a stick and the penny catechism. You can do one of two things about the conditioning that form of education gives you; you can kick against it, and turn it on its head – as writers like James Joyce did – or you can wallow in it. I wallowed because I loved it. It provided me with a world of colour, historical resonance, poetry and intellectual vigour way beyond anything else in my provincial Irish upbringing. And when as a teenager I came to England, I was lucky enough to be sent to a school where religious education was in the hands of two exceptionally gifted men. At a time when most teenagers are quite understandably rejecting the threadbare platitudes that often pass for Christianity, I was being made to read Kafka and Sartre and Camus and Wittgenstein and Ryle, I was being introduced to the critical study of the Bible, I was being shown that religion had something worth hearing to say about all the issues of life and death. So I went to university, and read theology and philosophy to begin with. And though I met and liked and talked through many long days and nights with people who did not believe, I never encountered anything that seemed half so rich or so satisfying as my inherited Catholicism. I married a Christian, and so never had to confront the problem of fundamental allegiance that being in love with a non-believer might have posed. Three years of research in church history only confirmed all this, and my satisfaction was bolstered by the willingness of many of the people I met to be influenced by me. I was not only religious, I was *successfully* religious.

In my last year or so as a student at Cambridge I was introduced to a blind man, a retired Anglican priest, who lived just outside the town. I used to cycle out once a week to read to him. He was a very remarkable person; despite his blindness he edited a magazine, and was at the centre of an ever-expanding circle of friends of every class, creed, colour and sex – he married a number of them off to each other! He was a life-giver, full of wisdom, which he disguised with a rather freakish, macabre sense of humour. In 1971 I moved away to my first job, and I just about kept in touch with him; and then in the following year I got news, very unexpectedly, that he had died. It turned out to be the most traumatic event of my life. Never before or since has anything so terrible happened to me. I still do not know why I was so affected, but in the weeks after his death I woke up night after night, drenched in icy sweat, swept by wave after wave of nauseating physical fear of death; my own, my wife's, our new-born son's. Not fear that somehow we might die *soon,* unexpectedly; just a horrifying realization that one day there would be nothing; that our hopes, our preoccupations, our beliefs would be simply brushed aside, shown up for the meaningless treadmill they had always been. And with the horror came the realization that God was gone; there was no God, and I had no faith. All the conditioning, all the arguments and emotional scaffolding I had built around and into my life were as if they had never been. I no longer believed, no longer even wanted to believe; I was absolutely mesmerized by this overwhelming perception of mortality. I had never been much good at prayer, and now more than ever prayer seemed hollow. I felt confused and embarrassed by my attempts to pray, like a man caught talking to himself in a railway carriage.

What I want to emphasize is that *intellectually* nothing had changed. The arguments for or against belief seemed neither stronger nor weaker to me than they had ever done before; I *could* still, and endlessly I *did,* put up a strong case for believing in God. Quite simply, it carried no weight for me. The death of my blind friend seemed the ultimate rebuttal. He was dead; everything, good or bad, would die.

I had encountered this awful annihilating blanket of death once before; but that had been safely between the covers of a book I had read as a sixth-former, Camus's *l'Etranger, The Outsider.* There is a horrifying scene towards the end of the novel where the Outsider is waiting for execution in the death cell, and he explains the mystery which has dominated the book so far, his own total deadness of feeling, his inability to love or to hate, to regret or to hope. A priest is trying to talk to him, and the Outsider, just for once, explodes.

> I hurled insults at him, I told him not to waste his rotten prayers on me; it was better to burn than to disappear . . . he seemed so cocksure, you see. And yet none of his certainties were worth one strand of a living woman's hair. It might look as if my hands were empty. Actually I was sure of myself, sure about everything, far surer than he. Sure of my present life and the death that was coming . . . all the time I'd been waiting for this present moment, for that dawn, tomorrow's or another day's, which was to justify me. Nothing had the least importance, and I knew quite well why. From the dark horizon of my future a sort of slow persistent breeze had been blowing towards me, all my life long, from the years that were to come. And on its way that breeze had levelled out all the ideas people tried to foist on me in the unreal years I was living through. What difference could they make to me, the death of others or a mother's love or his God. As a condemned man himself, couldn't he grasp what I meant by that dark wind blowing from my future?

Standing now in the full blast of that same dark wind, my plight had none of that appalling eloquence or clarity. But I felt myself confronted with the same issue. Were love and meaning to be flattened by my conviction that the world did not add up, that it had no significance greater than the sum of its parts? If people were ephemeral, were the things they lived by and for ephemeral? Looking at what had been lovable and admirable in my friend's life, could I just say that had been 'nice' and turn away? Could I say, in fact, 'death is stronger than love'?

I found I could not, and the implications of my inability to do so baffled me. I could find no way of holding on to the values of Christianity while denying the account Christianity gave of reality. It would not do to say that, yes, the world *was* a bleak place subject to inexorable material forces, and yet that one

might as well structure one's life by values like love and selfless-
ness and compassion, because they were really very attractive.
I did not see how righteousness could be reduced to some sort
of pleasant and useful hobby like carpentry or crocheting,
something to fill in the time till the hearse came to take me
away. And I could not make any sense of the idea of defeated
virtue for its own sake. I once saw an appalling newsreel of
the Russian invasion of Hungary, in which a man rushed into
the streets with a national flag, which he brandished defiantly
in the path of an oncoming tank, till it rolled over him with a
noise like crackling sweet-wrappings. Was goodness like that;
was *Jesus* like that? I found that I simply could not see righteousness as *pathetic,* a lost cause, like defeated Jacobite squires
drinking to the king over the water who would never come
into his own. I did not see how one could affirm the beatitudes,
and yet assert that in no circumstances whatever would the
meek inherit the earth.

All this time I had carried on going to Mass, though I didn't
know what I was doing there. And it was there, in its celebration of the death of Jesus (and what an extraordinary idea the
celebration of a death seemed), that I found something by which
I could establish some sort of bearing on my turmoil. For as I
knelt there rather numbly, week by week, it dawned on me that
the Mass began from the point at which I had now arrived.
Here, in a ritual grown commonplace to me by long acquain-
tance, there was an unblinking contemplation of all the ills of
humanity. Here it was acknowledged that men and women die,
often horribly, that good is defeated, that power crushes
tenderness, that lies swallow up the truth. And in the face of
that acknowledgement, in the face of the cross, the Mass
proclaimed a celebration, an affirmation of the unquenchable
life of love. Out of death – and not just the death of Jesus, but
out of *my* death, 'the masterful negation and collapse of all that
made *me* man' – it asserted our right to rejoice. It did so because
there had once been a man whose trust in the loving reality that
underlay the world was so total that in the face of his own
destruction he could still call that reality Father; whose death

was not an end to his loving, but the means of its infinite expansion. I saw that what was on offer here, true or false, was not an escape from my own mortality, for it began with a death. Karl Rahner says somewhere that 'when we look on the face of the Crucified we know that we are to be spared nothing'. What *was* on offer was an account of our living and dying which did justice to its urgency, and its fragility, and its lovableness; which affirmed that the forces that give warmth and worth to our existence have power in the dark places, even in death. And I knew I had to choose, between the bleak valueless world of the Outsider, and the world of human significance, where love and forgiveness and celebration were possibilities.

I do not have much recollection of the process by which I made my choice; except that, when it dawned on me that I had made it, it seemed not so much a choice as a gift. As I sat after Communion one Sunday, simply looking at the people walking up to the altar, I was quietly overwhelmed with an overflowing sense of companionship, of gratitude, of joy and, oddly, of pity. My mind filled up, quite literally filled up, with a single verse of the Psalms (26:8):

> Lord, how I love the beauty of your house, . . .
> and the place where your glory dwells . . .

There was no miraculous conviction. Perplexities and pain remained. I had and I have fewer certainties than before, and there are many areas of the faith that I gratefully and whole-heartedly accept which are opaque to me, like the idea of life after death. But now I know that faith is a direction, not a state of mind; states of mind change and veer about, but we can hold a direction. It is not in its essence a set of beliefs *about* anything, though it involves such beliefs. It is a loving and grateful openness to the gift of being. The difference between a believer and a non-believer is not that the believer has one more *item* in his mind, in his universe. It is that the believer is convinced that reality is to be trusted, that in spite of appearances the world is very good. When we respond to that good, we are not responding to something we have invented, or projected. Meaning is not at our beck and call, and neither is reality. When we try to talk *about* that reality we find ourselves talking *to* it, not in philosophy but in adoration, for it is inescapably Personal, and most luminously itself in the life and death of Jesus. Christians are those who find in that life and death an abounding fountain of joy and hope and life; who affirm and are content to affirm what he affirmed about God, because they find in that affirmation a realism which does justice to life in all its horror and all its glory. Not sad, high-minded men with a handful of high-minded, bleak ideals, but citizens of a world whose heart is love. We know in the way of Jesus, not a *law,* but a liberation into true humanity; the power to love, to belong to one another, to start again when things go wrong, to be grateful, to adore.

Every one of us, every human being, confronts at some time the collapse of meaning and direction in our lives – in anxiety, in illness, in unemployment or broken relationships, in all the forces that frustrate and diminish us as persons, and, at the last, in our own deaths. The Church has no pat answers to the dilemmas of existence, only a witness to what she knows. That under the mercy of God our perplexities, our failures, our betrayals, our limitations, can open into new freedoms, if we follow the way of Jesus. A century and a half ago, Coleridge wrote: 'Christianity is not a theory, or a speculation, but a Life; not a philosophy of life, but a Life, and a living process . . . Try it.' I don't know how to better that advice; like Coleridge, I have found life in the God of Abraham and Isaac and Jacob, like millions of others in every age, like the psalmist before us:

I love the Lord, for he has heard the cry of my appeal.
For he turned his ear to me
in the day when I called him.
They surrounded me, the snares of death, with the
    anguish of the tomb:
They caught me, sorrow and distress: I called on the
    Lord's name . . .

Turn back, my soul, to your rest, for the Lord has been
   good.
He has kept my soul from death, my eyes from tears,
and my feet from stumbling.
I will walk in the presence of the Lord,
in the land of the living. (Psalm 114)

A very fine
testimony

2

Confessions of a Cradle Catholic

There seems something fundamentally dishonest in a Catholic of my background and generation pretending to offer a detached, universally applicable account of the power or attraction of the Church. I did not choose to be a Catholic: for me Catholicism is something bred in the bone, as fundamental a part of my identity as my name or (especially) my nationality. I was born in 1947 in the Irish east coast town of Dundalk, a strongly nationalist community just south of the border. During the Troubles of the 1970s it would earn the nickname 'Dodge City' because it was the heart of IRA 'bandit country': my own family were ardent nationalists. They were also (though somewhat less ardently) Catholics: ours was an observant but not a particularly pious household.

Everyone went to Mass, and my mother and I sometimes attended Rosary, Sermon and Benediction on a weekday evening. Like everyone else, we ate fish on Fridays, we kept the fast days in Lent, we made popular novenas, to Our Lady of Perpetual Succour or St Gerard Majella at the local Redemptorist church (I was always baffled by the astonishing number of heavily pregnant women in the congregation) and we all had several stabs (in my case uniformly unsuccessful) at keeping the 'Nine First Fridays' – Confession and Communion on which, nine months in a row, guaranteed a holy death. But there were no collective family prayers in our house. My parents had devotional books, and owned rosaries, which they used at Mass, but though I often recited the Rosary and Litany of Loretto communally in the evenings, that was at the home of a close friend (son of the local undertaker) who had a pious mother. But the Rosary was by no means exclusively for the pious. My grandmother, a formidable, bespectacled and black bombazined Victorian, the dominant figure in all our lives, loved and feared in almost equal measure, was not a pious woman. For the last 20 years or more of her life she pleaded infirmity, and so far as I know never entered a church, though she often went out shopping locally. Instead, a curate came once a month to bring her Communion – the younger priests were said to compete for the privilege, so hilarious was her conversation. But, sleepless with old age, she prayed the rosary all night long, and kept a luminous statue of Our Lady of Lourdes on the mantlepiece of her bedroom (sleeping privileged alongside her, as I sometimes did, in her high brass bed, I was made uneasy by the statue's sickly phosphorescent glow). The sound of the rosary still calls up for me the childhood memory of waking to the loud tick of a tin alarm-clock in that utterly safe darkness, bathed in the smell of Sloane's Linament, and hearing my grandmother's muttered preamble – 'This one is for Tom, for Henry, for Molly, for Lily' – as she launched on yet another decade.

Almost everyone I knew was a Catholic, just as almost everyone I knew was poor. My grandmother, a British army widow, lived in a street built before Independence by the British Legion, and so had some Protestant friends: her own husband, my grandfather, had been an Ulster Presbyterian. But Protestants were exotics in our community, mostly middle class and so a cut above us anyway, unmolested but not fully comprehended, and thought of as definitely unIrish. For the rest, Catholicism was like breathing out and breathing in, part of the landscape, a given.

What did it give? A sense of the eternal verities, certainly, and a strong ritual framework for life's entrances and exits. When anyone in our street died, the children were rounded up and brought to the wake house to sprinkle holy water and say a prayer by the open coffin: I have vivid memories of a friend's young plump mother, reduced by cancer to a waxen doll, her stick fingers wound round with beads, her coffin filled with hair, but the strangeness and terror held in place, and at bay, by the familiarities of the *De Profundis* and the conventions of Catholic mourning. Funerals were communal events, the local graveyard a meeting-place. A mile or so outside the town on the main Dublin–Belfast road, funeral cortèges (there seemed so many of them) processed there at a slow walking pace, and the nation's traffic, such as it was in the 1950s, slowed behind them. The liturgy was, for the most part, without grace or decorum – Pius XII's wonderful renewal of the Holy Week ceremonies had not yet happened, or at any rate had not penetrated to our parish, and apart from the familiar Latin of *Tantum Ergo* and *O Salutaris* at Benediction (for sheer theatre and nostalgic power, my favourite service) we sang only sacherine nineteenth-century hymns to the Blessed Virgin or the Sacred Heart, and we set a special value on priests who could gallop through a Mass in 12 minutes flat.

But the rhythms of the liturgical year, though not much reflected upon, were as absolute a part of the calendar as winter fogs or leaves in autumn – palms and ashes (we children held up screws of paper on Ash Wednesday, into which the priest dropped pinches of spare ash, ostensibly for house-bound relatives, really to freshen up our glorious black smudges as the day wore on and they wore off): the smell of incense and the subtler but more pervasive smell of holy water (in my parish church it was kept in bulk in a zinc dustbin by the street door, and there was always someone there filling a bottle: what did people do with it – drink it, gargle? We seemed to get through gallons). There were stiff gold vestments at Easter or Christmas, purple in Lent, and an astonishing clapper device like a football rattle in place of the bells in Holy Week. First Communions and Confirmations were folk events, row upon row of girls in miniature wedding dresses and veils, the suited boys with sashes and bemedalled rosettes. In our working-class community it was an event eagerly awaited, because when it was your turn you went round the neighbours in your holy kit and they gave you money. And at your Confirmation, aged nine or so, you raised your right hand and, speaking after the bishop, solemnly took the pledge, renouncing alcoholic beverages.

My school was run by De La Salle Brothers, raw-boned, stubble-chinned celibates in shiny black cassocks, topped by bizarre stiff white tabs which jutted from the front rims of their hard dog-collars like the bleached tables of the law, and made your neck and chin sore just to look at them. Very few were local products: they came from Leitrim and Mayo and all points west, they were keen on hurling and pipe-smoking and the glories of Ireland, strenuous beaters to a man (some of the Brothers carried crook-handled canes in a special loop on the inside of their soutanes), few of them with much in the way of intellectual interests, yet decent enough for the most part, and it was they who took charge of our religious education. This consisted of teaching us to recite the Rosary, go to Confession, serve Mass, and get off by heart the Irish version of the penny catechism, which started with God ('Who is God?' 'God is our Father in heaven, the Creator and Sovereign Lord of all things') and human destiny ('Why did God make you?' 'God made me to know love and serve him in this life, and to be happy with him for ever in the next'), then worked its way through the ten commandments, the seven virtues (four cardinal, three theological) the seven corporal and spiritual works of mercy, the seven deadly sins, the seven sacraments (why did God make everything in sevens, we wondered: how many fingers and toes did he have?). I know them still: ultimate reality named and tagged, the moral structure of the universe set out for use in the pages of a soft-backed schoolbook: sorted.

Catholicism was certainty: papal infallibility over against the invincible ignorance of unfortunate Protestants (God help them, what did they know?) but also the calm and in retrospect breath-taking authority assumed by the clergy. Our parish priest was said to have put a stop to a clandestine strip club opened in the back room of a local bar by turning up late one evening, unannounced, armed with a stout ash-plant: men and women limped for weeks. This was holy Ireland, muscular version. But

Catholicism was also mystery: the competent mutter and movement of the priest at the altar, the words of power half-understood, the sense of being in touch, literally in touch, with holy things, with Holiness itself. The spotless starched linen of alb and corporal, the priest's fingers and thumb held tightly together all through the latter part of the Mass so that not the minutest crumb of the consecrated Host might be lost, a tight grip on the transmaterial: ritual and taboo, like the ban on eating or drinking even a drop of water from midnight the night before you went to Communion: rules which marked the presence of the Immensities.

And as part of the mystery, continuity too: underneath, but not far underneath, the doctrinal drilling, the repressed sexuality and the sternly regular sacramental observance which the nineteenth-century clergy had imposed on their peasant congregations, there was an older, rawer, folk Christianity, linked to the rock and water of hill and lake and well. Two miles from my home was the shrine of Foughart, legendary birth-place of St Brigid, whom I have since learned is perhaps a Christian sanitization of a Celtic goddess. The shrine had been modernized with a life-sized Calvary, concrete stations of the cross and garishly painted statues of Patrick and Brigid, and there was an annual pilgrimage or 'patron' there led by local clergy – my brother, an altar-boy, remembered the curate who had been ordered to preach, muttering on the way there, 'God in heaven, what'll I say to these people?'. But the real life of the shrine was a series of oddly shaped stones scattered round a stream. Here was the hole left when Brigid threw one of her eyes on it, plucked out to repel an importunate suitor: here were the marks left by her knees as she knelt all night on the rock. We bathed sore eyes there, and the arthritic knelt where she had knelt. In the ancient graveyard on the hill, the burial-place of Edward the Bruce, in the news a few years ago because the IRA left there the exhumed body of one of their long lost victims, there was her holy well, the thorn bush beside it aflutter with the rags and ribbons tied by the devout.

All that came to an end for me in June 1960, when the family emigrated to England. The Vatican Council was in session, and for anyone interested in theology, as I was rapidly learning to be, it was an intoxicating period. Under the influence of superb religious education at my Catholic grammar school (our RS master, a priest, went on to be the first Catholic professor of theology in an English university since the Reformation) my Catholicism changed beyond recognition. I shed my inherited Ultramontanism, became (briefly) a zealot for change, put folk religion behind me. And 40 years on, that sort of Catholicism seems gone for most other people too, even for those who live still in Ireland, where not only has the Council transformed the ethos and worship of Catholicism, but where, for quite other reasons, the Church has so spectacularly begun to lose its grip upon the minds and hearts of the Irish. In recent years we have seen to the full the dark side of Christianity when it shrinks to becoming the ideology and the possession of a nation: Ireland apart, in the Balkans, Orthodox Serb and Catholic Croat have each perpetrated atrocity and ethnic cleansing in the interests of the so-called integrity of a Christian people. We are rightly suspicious of national Christianity.

The Church is One, Holy, Catholic, Apostolic, and I have come to see that the witness of the Church of my childhood to unity, holiness, catholicity, apostolicity, was very imperfect indeed. The unity we valued as a Catholic people was narrow and exclusive, a self-definition over against the Protestant other. It was not, I think, actively discriminatory or ill-willed, as Protestantism seemed to us to be towards Catholics in the North. Simply, our religion had no place for the other: they did not feature in the story we told about who we were. As church scandal follows scandal in the modern Irish press, and the media seize gleefully on horror stories of brutality to orphans and unmarried mothers, or of abusive clergy and teachers, we realize too, now, how hollow the notion of Holy Ireland could often be. Our conception of Catholicity was better based, and stemmed from our pride in belonging to Latin, Roman, Christianity, though it too was part of our nationalism. England, we thought, had apostatized, but the Irish had always been faithful to Rome. Ireland might be sneered at as backward, provincial, but in religion at least we were citizens of no mean city, and it was Protestantism which seemed to us provincial.

From this side of the Council, we can see that even *Romanitas* has severe limitations as an expression of Christian universality. The regimented discipline of Rome, the exclusive use of Latin in the liturgy, seemed then the epitome of that universalism. The Church was an army, spread across the world, moving to a single drumbeat, following a single law, speaking with a single voice: it was as if the Holy Spirit had inspired the Apostles to speak Latin, and not the myriad tongues of the diaspora, on the day of Pentecost. But we have come to value diversity at least as much as uniformity as a potent sign of the Church's universal mission. And that indeed is the point: all these marks of the true Church are part, not so much of what she already is, as of what she is called to be. Catholics before the Council often spoke as if the visible Church had already achieved perfect unity, holiness, catholicity, apostolicity. These were characteristics we Catholics had, locked, strapped and sorted, and they were ours alone. But in fact the unity, holiness and universality of the Church belong to her perfection, they lie ahead of the Church, '*perigrinantem in terra*' as the Mass says, wandering here on earth, and not behind her.

All this I know, indeed passionately feel. Why is it then, that as I grow older, and after 35 years of studying and teaching the theology and history of the Church, I find myself living more and more out of resources acquired not in the lecture room or library, nor even at the post-Conciliar liturgy, but in the narrow Catholicism of my 1950s childhood, warts and all? To answer that question fully would no doubt require a descent into my subconscious and my family history for which this is decidedly not the place. But it springs too, from a growing appreciation of just how much of the essence of Catholicism my provincial Irish childhood transmitted to me. For all its apparent narrowness, it bore stronger witness than many modern forms of Catholicism to realities which have come to seem to me infinitely precious. Its ritual absolutes and rules look legalistic, rubric-mad today: but they spoke with a sure confidence of the sacramentality of life, the rootedness of the sacred not in pious feelings or 'spirituality', not in our heads or even exclusively our hearts, but in the gritty and messy realities of life, birth and death, water and stone and fire, bread and wine. The matter-of-fact *ex opere operato* confidence of our ritual world assured us that God was real, with a reality that did not depend on what we thought or how we felt about it. And its ritual contacts with the remote past, its shrines and graveyards and wells, helped us locate our little lives within longer and wider continuities: the railwaymen and shoemakers and labourers of 1950s Dundalk were more dignified as human beings because of the sense of their companionship with the holy dead. In our throw-away society, where people live disposable lives in increasing social isolation, that is an affirmation worth repeating.

Even the pat certainties of the Catechism have come to mean a good deal to me. I no longer think that you can find the answers to the problems of life and death, faith and doubt, neatly stitched up in a schoolbook. But at the heart of the Catholic faith is a confidence that meaning and value are not arbitrary constructs, that the most fundamental human instincts about right and wrong, about human flourishing and human misery, are rooted in the pattern of creation itself, and in God's self-disclosure in grace and revelation. We can believe, and hope, and love, because God has drawn near to us, in the order of nature, in the fabric of human society and morality, in the religious aspirations of all people in all places, and above all in the history of Israel and in the person of Christ. For all its limitations and simplifications, the Catechism was a coded form of a rich collective wisdom, handed on and received with joy, which went back through the lives and teaching of the saints, to Aquinas, to Augustine, to the apostles themselves. The intellectual confidence that, despite all its mystery, and miseries, and terrors, the world is a place where we belong, whose meaning and purpose we can know, by the force of reason and by the light of faith, is one of the foundation stones of Catholic Chris-

tianity, and I realize now that I was taught it, parrot-fashion, by
the De la Salle Brothers.

The clerical authoritarianism of the Church of the 1950s
now looks what it was, a drastic and distorted overdevelopment
of one element of the Church's historical particularity at the
expense of other equally important dimensions, like the role of
prophecy or the dignity of the laity. I do not now believe that
God's truth is to be received unquestioningly from the mouths
of clergymen, whether they be popes or, more frighteningly,
the parish priests of pre-Conciliar Ireland. But if we believe in
the reality of revelation, and if we believe that the Church is
entrusted with it, then we have to give a concrete meaning and
form to that confidence. We cannot indefinitely postpone our
obedience and response to the truth, as it seems to me many
forms of liberal protestantism tend to do. If the Church has the
gospel of truth, *someone, somewhere*, has to be trusted to say what
it is, and to call on us to receive it. That process seems to me
now more complex and less simplistically hierarchical than we
imagined in 1950, but the essence of what we believed in 1950
seems to me both true, and precious. A Church without real
authority is not the Church at all. We receive and proclaim the
Catholic faith which comes to us from the apostles, we do not
invent it: the Brothers, and my grandmother, knew that too.

3

Popular Religion

Two large framed and matching coloured prints hung on the back wall of the bedroom I shared with my brothers in Ireland in the 1950s. They depicted the Sacred Heart of Jesus and the Immaculate Heart of Mary: life-sized half-length figures of Jesus and Mary gazed mesmerically down, drawing back their cloaks (red for Jesus, blue for Mary) in order to point to luridly veined and glistening hearts, improbably placed in the centre of their chests and ghosting through their snow-white tunics, ringed and pierced with thorns (in Mary's case with roses), blazing with flames like coronets of unruly red hair, and each topped by a cross. They had, I think, been given to my parents as a wedding present – in Ireland at that time marriage was sometimes jokingly described as a contract between a man, a woman and a picture of the Sacred Heart. The prints, with their acid chemical colours and excruciating detail, were almost nightmarishly vivid, and I was a devout child: each morning and night I knelt before them to say my prayers, much taken with the fact that their eyes appeared to follow me round the room.

I have since realized that I was in fact probably more than a little afraid of them. At any rate, their doleful and unsleeping eyes, moist, reproachful, appealing, continued to haunt my imagination long after the pictures themselves had been disposed of, when my family moved to England in the early 1960s. But these images were utterly characteristic domestic expressions of a form of Catholicism, in which special devotions loomed large – to the Immaculate Heart of Mary, to St Joseph (to secure a happy death), to our Guardian Angels, to the Holy Infant of Prague, to our Lady of Perpetual Succour, to the Immaculate Conception, above all to the Sacred Heart of Jesus. Every church had a statue of the Sacred Heart, every house and sometimes every room in every house had a picture. My father was a Pioneer, a teetotaller vowed to total abstention from alcohol in reparation to the Sacred Heart for the evils caused by drunkenness. To alert people not to offer him drinks, he wore an enamelled lapel badge, which had on it an emblem of the Sacred Heart.

The prayer book my family took to Mass each Sunday was called the *Treasury of the Sacred Heart*. Originally a Victorian compilation, it was endlessly reprinted till the 1950s, and was designed as a *vade-mecum* of the pious life. It provided forms of morning and evening prayer, preparation for Confession, the hymns and prayers for benediction, a Latin text and English translation of the ordinary of the Mass, and the Sunday epistles and gospels in English. But the bulk of the book was taken up with a host of special devotions: Acts of Reparation to the Sacred Heart, together with a list of the promises made by Jesus to the seventeenth-century French nun who had originally popularized the devotion: the Stations of the Cross: a series of Litanies – of the Holy Name, the Sacred Heart, the Litany of Loretto: a variety of rosaries – the Rosary of the Blessed Virgin, the Rosary of the Holy Name, the Rosary of the Precious Blood, the Rosary of the Seven Dolours: a variety of Novenas, or schemes of prayer spread over nine days, or weeks, or months – in honour of the Guardian Angels, or St Joseph, St Patrick, St Brigid, St Dominic, and of course the Sacred Heart of Jesus. There were a series, too, of privileged and indulgenced prayers – the 'En Ego', to be said after Communion before a crucifix, the 'Memorare' to the Virgin, the 'morning offering', dedicating the day to Jesus through the most pure heart of Mary.

Most of these prayers and devotions carried indulgences, spiritual benefits granted by the pope and remitting penance or time in purgatory, mysteriously calculated in days or years – 500 days for the prayer to Jesus, Mary and Joseph for a happy death, 'plenary' or total in the case of the 'En Ego'. And some of these prayers and devotions carried more concrete guarantees: peace in the family and a blessing on the house where a picture of the Sacred Heart was displayed, guaranteed access to a priest and the last sacraments at the hour of death for those who successfully completed the 'nine first Fridays' (Confession and Communion at Mass on the first Fridays of nine consecutive months). Devout daily recitation for a month of the immensely long 'Thirty Days Prayer to the Blessed Virgin Mary in honour of the Sacred Heart of Jesus' carried the promise that 'we may hope to obtain any lawful request', a carefully inexplicit formula which did not prevent the highest hopes being placed on the prayer itself.

And our oleographs of the Sacred and Immaculate Hearts were just two in a gallery of special images. We also had statues of both the Sacred Heart and the Immaculate Conception, and a battered statue of the Infant of Prague, to me at the time a baffling representation of the child Jesus, dressed in a jewelled cope and oriental-looking crown, one hand raised in blessing, the other holding a jewelled orb. In some places this image was believed to guarantee good weather if left on the doorstep overnight, but not in our rain-sodden town, sandwiched between mountains and sea, and rarely dry.

These domestic pieties, available to any devotee with the appropriate prayer book or holy statue or picture, were part of a wider religious culture in which devotions provided the principal texture and warmth of popular Catholicism. The De La Salle Brothers who ran my school were the sponsors of a devotional association called the Archconfraternity of the Divine Child: we regularly assembled in the school hall (which doubled as the local cinema) for communal prayers in front of a life-sized statue of the child Jesus. The Redemptorist Fathers, who ran the parish church near the railway works, were the sponsors of an annual novena to St Gerard Majella, much patronized by pregnant women, and they also ran a continuous or perpetual novena to Our Lady of Perpetual Succour, a devotion linked to a much-reproduced fifteenth-century

Cretan Icon of the Virgin and Child flanked by angels holding the instruments of the passion, which was kept in the Order's mother-church in Rome. At school we were encouraged to take up other specially privileged devotional practices – like many of my contemporaries I joined the Confraternity of Our Lady of Mount Carmel, and wore the 'brown scapular', two small, itchy woollen squares, worn suspended back and front round the neck under one's clothing. I also joined the Legion of Mary, and attended the prayer meetings of the local group (called a *Praesidium*), gathered round an improvized altar in the living-room of one of the lay teachers at my school, on which was placed a statue of the Immaculate Conception flanked by candles, and a strange free-standing object called a *Vexillum*, which was a miniature Roman legionary standard surmounting a marble ball, and inscribed with a passage from the Old Testament: 'Who is she who comes forth fair as the moon, bright as the sun, terrible as an army with banners?' This exotic symbol, the mysterious verses applied to Mary, and the idealistic solidarity of the group, were all part of the attraction of membership of the Legion.

All these were voluntary activities, undertaken by pious individuals. But all the parish churches in the town staged well-attended Stations of the Cross in Lent, and May and October Devotions, Marian services which normally took the form of Rosary, Sermon and Benediction, the sermons anecdotal accounts of the miracles of the Virgin and her power to rescue sinners at the hour of death. Nothing in them would have been out of place a century or so earlier, and indeed I have since recognized some of the stories we were told, in classic source-books like St Alphonsus Ligouri's *The Glories of Mary*. Most of the devotions we practised were in fact Baroque in origin, going back to the Italian or French seventeenth and eighteenth century, and by the same token, St Alphonsus was the principal author drawn on by the editors of the *Treasury of the Sacred Heart*. And this sort of piety was entirely characteristic of post-Tridentine Catholicism. Pre-Conciliar Ireland, the most observant Catholic country in the world, no doubt cultivated this type of Catholicism in almost chemical purity, but the devotional world I grew up in was by no means an exclusively Irish phenomenon. Precisely the same sort of piety was, *mutatis mutandi*, observed by Catholics from Poland to Peru.

Maybe in Poland or Peru, among other places, this sort of piety still thrives. By and large, however, and especially in Western Europe and the USA, though individual components of the pre-Conciliar devotional world survive, its overall close-knit unity of texture and imaginative hold have weakened and in many places disappeared. This should be no surprise, for a fundamentally negative account of such piety lay at the very roots of the liturgical revival, and of the 'new theology' which shaped so much of the liturgical and spiritual revolution inaugurated by the Second Vatican Council. Two generations of liturgical pioneers, from Odo Casel to Joseph Jungmann and Louis Bouyer, explained the emergence of this devotional world in the Middle Ages as a sign of decadence, an unsatisfactory compensation for the alienation of the laity from the liturgy, and from the sacramental participation in the mystery of salvation which the liturgy offered.

After the Patristic period, they believed, the laity had been increasingly shut out of their birthright of full and active participation in the liturgy – the words of the Mass and other sacraments were in Latin, not the vernacular, and the laity seldom received Communion. At Mass they became spectators at a show which they barely understood: to make sense of what they saw, the actions of the Mass were allegorized as reminders of the stages of the passion, and memory and drama became the principal ways in which ordinary people encountered the work of redemption. The Franciscan order in particular encouraged lay people to put sorrowing meditation on the minutest details of the passion and death of Jesus at the heart of their religious lives, and a high value was placed on devotional tears, on feeling compassion for Christ's sufferings, fellow-feeling with the grieving Mary. In place of the sacramental encounter with the risen and transforming Christ which faithful participation in the liturgy brought, sentiment and emotion took over. The

Paschal mystery became something to be grasped inside one's head, instead of a transforming reality which raises and transforms us through encounter and communion.

Louis Bouyer indeed considered that the emotional piety of the Middle Ages – the lamentations over the dead Christ embodied in the Way of the Cross or statues of the *Pietà* or the Man of Sorrows, or the emergence of the devotion to the Sacred Heart as a refinement of earlier devotion to the five wounds of Jesus – had prepared the way for Protestantism, by substituting a sentimental emphasis on religious 'experience' in place of what Bouyer called 'the sober mysticism, completely grounded in faith, of the great Christian Tradition', and above all enshrined in the liturgy. He and his colleagues particularly deplored the modern devotion to the Sacred Heart, with its piety of 'reparation' for sins against Christ, as if the death of Jesus was a defeat for which the Son of God needed comfort or consolation, instead of the great moment of his victory and glorification, transforming and nourishing us and the whole cosmos into resurrection life through the communion of the liturgy. For Bouyer and his associates, the devotional world I have been describing, far from being symptomatic of vigour and commitment, was instead the hectic fever of a sick Christianity, desperately in need of the healing medicine of liturgical renewal.

The historical analysis offered by Bouyer and others was certainly correct as far as it went, and their unease with the devotional world of the pre-Conciliar Church was well founded. Catholic Christianity offers assurance of salvation and nourishes its children in the Christian life primarily through the proclamation of God's word and by sacramental encounter with Christ in the communal celebration of the liturgy. The devotions of the Middle Ages and Baroque period were sometimes, to put it mildly, rather precariously rooted in the Bible, and looked for alternative forms of assurance – privileged prayers and pious acts validated by legendary visions, in which God or Mary or the saints offered special guarantees or promised special efficacy to particular acts or forms of words.

The practice of Indulgences did at least help root this quest for guaranteed efficacy in the corporate and liturgical life of the Church. The whole ethos of miraculous promises or special guarantees which often attached to such devotions, however, opened the way to a merely magical or mechanistic understanding of the life of prayer, and ran the risk of locating the most deeply felt aspects of the religious life of the laity in private emotion, outside the liturgy, and outside the corporate experience of the whole worshipping community.

It is no surprise, then, that since the Council such devotions have dwindled away and in fact have sometimes been actively discouraged. There are fewer lurid statues in home and church, fewer venerable devotional practices attracting crowds in Lent or May or October, fewer novenas, medals, scapulars. But corrective reactions have a habit of swinging to opposite extremes. If much of the devotional life of the pre-Conciliar world was born from liturgical deprivation, and was indeed a form of compensation, much also was in fact a perfectly legitimate and healthy contemplative exercise, which helped lay people internalize and extend in practical ways the work of the liturgy within them. The explanation of all this devotional growth as a form of decadence which the liturgical pioneers offered relied on too simplistic a narrative. Devotional focus on particular aspects or actors within the Christian story did not begin as medieval decadence set in, but goes back to the earliest eras of Christianity. People need to brood over and digest the things that feed them. To elaborate and extend specific aspects of the Gospel story – the birth or infancy of Christ, the events of Calvary or the resurrection appearances – can enhance rather than detract from our engagement with the liturgy.

In his great book *Life and Liturgy*, still worth reading 50 years on, Bouyer warned against simply jettisoning the devotional developments of the medieval and Baroque period, whatever their origin. These too had become part of the shaping experience of Catholic tradition: if they were unliturgical or anti-liturgical, they should be reformed and reintegrated into a liturgical framework. Bouyer singled out devotion to the infant

Jesus and to the Blessed Sacrament in the Tabernacle as potentially anti-liturgical practices which could in fact become
profound meditations on the mysteries revealed in the liturgy.
The Child in the Manger could be approached not as the sentimental focus of human affection for babies, which it sometimes
was, but as the embodiment and assurance of the manifestation
of God in the mystery of the Incarnation which the liturgy
interprets and mediates to us. Visits to the Blessed Sacrament
need not be conversations with Christ imagined as a hidden
though powerful human friend, or a substitute for
Communion, but can be an affirmation, in 'the permanence of
the consecrated bread' of the reality and power of every
eucharistic celebration, the abiding sign of our nourishment and
transformation in the Mass.

Bouyer specially singled out the Rosary as the most liturgically positive of all popular devotions. It is hard to say whether
or not he had his tongue in his cheek. He was writing in the
mid-1950s: very soon, the recitation of the Rosary at Mass
would become the symbol *par excellence* of what was sometimes
scathingly referred to as 'bog-irish Catholicism', a prime
symptom of an unreconstructedly pre-Conciliar and non-
participatory folk religion. Bouyer, by contrast, thought the
15 mysteries of the Rosary in their simplicity and evangelical
purity 'an easy way of extending liturgical contemplation
throughout the whole of daily life . . . of bringing the whole of
our life continually back to its heavenly source'. If such
devotion ceased to be practised or thought of as an alternative
to liturgical involvement, and was instead replaced within the
context of a liturgically centred Catholicism, he thought, it
could augment and deepen appreciation of the reality
celebrated within the liturgy.

Two generations on, we can perhaps take up Bouyer's
invitation to repristinate rather than to reject the devotional
tradition with greater sympathy and enthusiasm than seemed
possible in the immediate and heady aftermath of the Council.
Many Catholics then felt impatience and scorn for the 'folk'
religion of the past, and believed that everything needed to

nourish the Christian life would be found within the new experience of the vernacular Mass. That, no doubt, is true, but we have a better sense now than then of the need to pause to explore, reflect on and deepen the themes of the liturgy, to let single moments or emphases blossom within us, and to give ourselves space and context so that can happen. Some devotions, of course, are so much the products of very particular eras and attitudes that it is hard to imagine their revival. Probably few devotees of the Child of Prague, for example, have been aware that the original wax image was a votive offering given to the church in Prague which was confiscated from the Lutherans and rededicated to Our Lady of Victories to celebrate the defeat of Protestantism at the outbreak of the Thirty Years War. Knowing that, however, it is hard to see how such an image could be repristinated for an ecumenical age.

But the past can surprise us. Despite his positive attitude to such devotions as the Rosary, Bouyer had serious reservations about the devotion to the Sacred Heart, a Baroque aberration which he thought would be hard to reconcile with a renewed liturgy. Yet an enthusiastically post-Conciliar priest in a difficult inner-city parish once told me that whenever he had the opportunity to celebrate Mass in people's homes or workplaces, especially when dealing with the unchurched or semi-detached, he invariably used the readings and prayers from the liturgy of Feast of the Sacred Heart, since their overwhelming emphasis on the love and tenderness of God eloquently and unforgettably expressed the very heart of the Gospel. After the Council we were often as a community puritanically suspicious of symbolism, ideologically impatient of the poetry of our inherited tradition, and convinced that those traditions had too often been shaped by bad theology. That was probably true enough, but it is part of the providence of God that the Church is usually more reliable on its knees than at the lecture podium. Our predecessors often got the theological formulae wrong, as we in our turn will no doubt do: but they knew how to pray. We can still learn from them.

I preached at Oscott R/c College at the Feast of the Sacred Heart and carried like "when I survey the Wondrous Cross". For me his moving Experience.

4

May Thoughts on Mary

May is Mary's Month, and I
Muse at that and wonder why.

Gerard Manley Hopkins, whose poem 'May Magnificat' opens
with these lines, might not have mused at all had he been
writing nowadays, instead of in 1878. One of the most striking
developments in post-Conciliar Catholicism has been the way
in which Marian piety has simply ceased to feature as a vital
dimension of their faith for a growing number of people. In
many English Catholic churches this May, traditional devotion
to Mary will be honoured more in the breach than in the
observance. This in itself has perhaps no great importance: the
familiar May devotions are in fact a fairly recent development,
initiated by an eighteenth-century Jesuit to promote chastity
among unruly students in Rome: there is nothing sacrosanct
about them.

Yet the comparative absence of a Marian element in the lives
of individual Christians, and in the corporate liturgical life of the
Church, is surely a matter for concern. For at least 1,500 years
the figure of the Mother of the Lord has been so central within
Catholicism, East and West, that some sort of living Mariology
must be judged one of its essential features, and not a devotional
optional extra. At its simplest and most obvious, the figure of
the Madonna cradling her child on her breast has placed at the
centre of our experience of the grace of God an unforgettable
image of human tenderness and nurture. In its light, the cross is

more readily understood as an act of love. We can think of God and his actions in terms of gentleness, vulnerability and growth, as well as in terms of power, judgement and perfection. This has been abundantly reflected in Christian art, and in the prayer-life of Christians, where prayer to Mary has often been one of the ways in which an overauthoritarian and judgemental perception of God has been avoided or compensated for.

In part the trouble is an exegetical failure, confusion and uncertainty about how to 'place' Mary within a more self-consciously scriptural Christianity. Greater awareness of the Bible among Catholics has led to uncertainties about Mary's cult, springing from such things as the apparent discrepancy between the comparatively small amount of space devoted to her in the New Testament on the one hand, and the dominance of her place in Catholic piety on the other. Moreover, the elements which have been most notable in recent Marian piety – emphasis on her purity, or on doctrines like the Assumption – have not always been those which are most evident within the scriptural material. And there is also a problem for many modern Christians in handling the mythic and poetic aspects of the cult of Mary. Many Catholics confronted with a text like the Litany of Loretto, with its beautiful but mysterious chain of titles – Ark of the Covenant, Tower of Ivory, Tower of David, Mystical Rose, and so on – simply do not know what to make of it.

But the apparent rejection or neglect of the cult of Mary springs also from a deeper and more fundamental unease. We are now more aware than before of the cultural particularity of different forms of Christian cult, and of the role of pieties both as expressions of and shapers of our attitudes to the world around us. One of the best poets writing in English, Seamus Heaney, is a Catholic brought up in County Derry in the 1940s and 1950s. He has returned in his writings time and again to the Marian, feminine character of Northern Irish Catholicism, a Christianity formed by the family Rosary and the Litany of Loretto, mournful, politically passive, turning its adherents into those who 'stoop along', 'one of the venerators', in sharp contrast to the masculine, aggressive and dominating religion of the Protestant settlers. The contrast is no doubt over-simple, and laden with assumptions about sex and gender which might be challenged, but it touches on a dimension of the cult of Mary as it was actually practised in these islands which may help to explain its present eclipse.

We can perhaps best approach this issue by looking at the section of hymns to Mary in the Westminster hymnal (1st edition, 1912), many of which were familiar to every British Catholic until the 1960s. There were 30 hymns to Our Lady in all, of which ten were translations either of the breviary hymns for the office of Our Lady, or from Latin devotional poems on her feast days: these translations were not great poetry, but taken as a whole they presented a balanced and essentially scriptural and patristic Mariology. Of the remaining 20 hymns, no fewer than ten were by the Victorian Oratorian priest, Fr Faber, and most of the rest were by Victorian writers who shared with Faber a florid and emotional Marian piety, perhaps best summed up by the habit Faber and his friends had of referring to the Blessed Virgin as 'Mama'.

The theology of these hymns is derived from a distinctive reading of the scene in the Gospel of St John when Jesus from the cross gives Mary to the beloved disciple as Mother. For Faber and his fellow hymnodists, Mary was supremely the Mother given in the darkness of a world which has crucified her Son. She is light where all else, including the Christian devotee, is darkness; she is pure where all else is filthy; she can console when all else is misery and despair.

O purest of creatures, sweet Mother! sweet Maid!
The one spotless womb wherein Jesus was laid!
Dark night has come down on us Mother, and we
Look out for thy shining, sweet Star of the Sea.

Deep night has come down on this rough-spoken world,
And the banners of darkness are boldly unfurled:
And the tempest-tossed Church – all her eyes are on thee,
They look to thy shining, sweet Star of the Sea.

Life, in these hymns, is nasty, brutish and short, and Mary the only comfort:

> Though poverty and work and woe
> The masters of my life must be
> When times are worst, who does not know
> Darkness is light with love of thee.

The client of Mary, too, is nasty and brutish, and stands under the judgement of God:

> See how, ungrateful sinners
> We stand before thy Son;
> His loving heart upbraids us
> The evil we have done.
> But if thou wilt appease Him,
> Speak for us but one word;
> For thus thou canst obtain us
> The pardon of the Lord.

All of these emphases, of course, have a long pedigree, and were by no means the invention of the Victorians. But they had a peculiar force within a piety which did not seek to balance them against different and more positive perceptions of the meaning and role of Mary. In particular, they depended for much of their emotional force on a *contrast* between Mary and the ordinary Christian, the contrast between pure and defiled, good and bad. The sinner approaching Mary never did so as like approaching like, but always the prodigal creeping shame-faced to a long-suffering, saintly and neglected mother.

> See at thy feet a sinner
> Groaning and weeping sore –
> Ah! throw thy mantle o'er me
> And let me stray no more.

This sort of perception clearly reflects a vivid sense of the reality of sin. But knowledge of one's own sinfulness, and a relentless harping on one's own vileness and unworthiness, are not at all the same thing, just as helpless guilt and true repentance are poles apart. The continual insistence in these hymns on the contrast between the purity and beauty of Mary on the one hand, and the vileness and degradation of the sinner on the other (often more or less explicitly associated with sexuality, since the focus of Mary's spiritual beauty was her chastity) probably also fostered a sense of alienation from self, a damaging loss of the sense of one's human and Christian dignity and potential, which may at times have hampered true repentance.

That inner alienation was paralleled by a disengagement from external as well as inner reality. The client of Mary in these hymns was presented as ill at ease in the world: an exile, lonely, at odds with all around him or her.

> Ave Maria! the night shades are falling,
> Softly our voices arise unto thee,
> Earth's lonely exiles for succour are calling,
> Sinless and beautiful, Star of the Sea.

Jews, Christians and Muslims have of course always shared the insight that for all those with faith, all the children of Abraham, life is a pilgrimage. They have accordingly emphasized the necessarily provisional character of commitment to any kingdom other than the Kingdom of God. But I think that something rather different was going on in these hymns, and that they represent a distinctive and rather peculiar sociology and politics. The world of these hymns is one in which 'the banners of darkness are boldly unfurled' against the 'tempest-tossed Church'. In this world, the devotee of Mary is beset by enemies, who hate goodness and purity, who hate the Church.

> O teach me, Holy Mary
> A loving song to frame,
> When wicked men blaspheme thee
> To love and bless thy name.

The world in which these hymns were first sung was perhaps a world in which it seemed plausible to think that 'wicked men blaspheme thee', whether the 'wicked men' were secularist soldiers in the French Revolution or the Italian Risorgimento, trampling holy images and looting the churches, or the editors of anti-Catholic newspapers, or to be found on the wrong side in the faction fights between Catholic and Protestant, Green and Orange, in the streets of Victorian Liverpool, Manchester and Glasgow.

But there was behind this whole Marian piety a profounder alienation, a sense that in the modern world the Christian had no role except that of denunciation. These were hymns for people without votes, or for those who disapproved of the states in which votes might be used. And much Marian devotion has had a disturbingly anti-democratic dimension to it. Nineteenth- and twentieth-century Marian piety has had a consistently world-renouncing and apocalyptic strain, in which the forces of evil are located not only in the heart of the Christian, but in the visible forces of Anti-Christ, identifiable 'wicked men' who stood over against the Church. Notoriously, the Virgin of Fatima was emphatically presented as a Cold Warrior, her message a fear-laden denunciation of Communism, laced with calls for Rosary Crusades as a counter-balance to ominous threats of nuclear war. Communist Russia was Mary's enemy, and so all those who combated Communism were her friends. I recall vividly as a boy in Ireland in the 1950s reading pious pamphlets in which the apparition at Fatima was explicitly associated with support for right-wing politics in the Iberian peninsula, a celestial endorsement of the regimes of Salazar and Franco.

I am not of course suggesting that everyone with a devotion to Mary before 1960 (or since) was a Fascist: but I do want to suggest that the conventional forms of Marian devotion – the rhetoric of the hymns and prayers addressed to her, the selection of her attributes and privileges which were singled out for attention, and the cult stories associated with her pilgrimages – were often pressed into service to endorse social and political attitudes, and modes of self-perception and self-evaluation, which now seem alien and distasteful to many Christians. There is of course much more to the matter than this, and I myself would not want to discount the genuinely prophetic element within even this flawed Marian tradition. But I have no doubt that (sometimes subliminal) discomfort with such attitudes is partly responsible for the widespread loss of confidence in traditional Mariology, and that any new and healthy Marian piety will need to reorientate itself in order to free itself from this particular cultural, political and psychological heritage.

The Second Vatican Council set the agenda for precisely this sort of reorientation by placing what it had to say about Mary within the context of its teaching on the Church. Mary is of course a unique figure, with a unique role in the salvation of the world. But her uniqueness is capable of being understood either exclusively, or inclusively. Where post-medieval Mariology often emphasized Mary's difference from every other Christian, her purity contrasting with our filth, her powerful intercession contrasting with our helplessness, the Council, following the mainstream of patristic and early medieval exegesis, emphasized her role as type and model for the Church, and each of its members. Thus her excellences and privileges, like her assumption into heaven, were not alienating measures of her distance from us, but pledges of the dignity which awaits us all, and which, in grace, is already taking shape within us.

Behind this dramatic change of emphasis lies an exegetical shift from the Gospel of St John to that of St Luke. Mary in St John's Gospel is of course also an inclusive and representative figure, but it was easy to understand it differently, to see her intercession at Cana or her maternal role at the cross as being *different from* in the sense of being *over against* that of all others. The Mary of Luke is less easy to misunderstand, and Catholic exegesis had constantly seen her *'fiat'* at the Annunciation, for all its momentous uniqueness, as the model of every believer's response to the call of God. In this perspective Mary is still a light to guide, but her light is a measure not of our darkness, but of the glory promised to all the saints.

This of course is no new perception. Julian of Norwich in the fourteenth century understood it well: in the eleventh of her Revelations God shewed her the Blessed Virgin, and the 'high, marvellous and singular love' he has for 'this sweet maiden, his blessed Mother'. But Julian immediately added that in Mary 'our Lord speaks to all mankind that shall be saved as it were all to one person, as if he said "Do you want to see in Her how you are loved?"' And Julian adds in commentary that in contemplating the virtues of Mary, her truth, her wisdom and her love, 'I may learn to know *myself* and reverently fear my God.'

The contrast between this positive and inclusive understanding of Mary's place and that of nineteenth-century and early-twentieth-century Mariology is obvious. Its potential as an element in a renewed Mariology for our time is also clear. Another and equally startling contrast with much pre-Conciliar Mariology has emerged in recent reflection on the significance of Our Lady's great hymn of praise to God, the Magnificat. Because it is recited so often, daily in the divine office, it is a text whose implications often pass unnoticed. Its rhetoric is that of the world turned upside down – the hungry fed, the rich sent empty away, the kings dethroned, the poor and oppressed raised up.

Nineteenth-century Mariology usually spiritualized these promises: the enemies to be toppled were not earthly tyrants, they were heresies and errors, or personal sins. Alternatively, the mighty on their thrones might be identified with the enemies of the Church (in the twentieth century, Soviet Communism), and the Magnificat treated as a promise of the triumph of the institutional Church. The text was emphatically not read as having a bearing on social justice more generally, and in a Mariology which endorsed right-wing regimes so long as they were Catholic, the text could be recited by stony-faced *generalisimos* without a qualm. A re-reading of St Luke's Gospel by liberation theologians has changed all that. The Christ of St Luke comes to 'preach good news to the poor, to proclaim release to captives, liberty to those oppressed' (Luke 4:18), and they have insisted that this proclamation is not to be spiritualized into harmlessness. In this light, Mary's song becomes a manifesto for the justice already erupting into the present world order, though its fulfilment will only be complete in the Kingdom, and Mary herself becomes a representative figure, a source of hope and strength for all who struggle for freedom from oppression. This is a development which has been commended and urged not only by John Paul II but by Paul VI, who wrote in his encyclical *Marialis Cultus* that:

> Mary . . . was anything but a passive, submissive woman, pious to the point of being out of contact with reality. No, here was a woman who did not hesitate to assert that God is the avenger of the oppressed, that he topples the mighty of this world from their thrones: in Mary we recognize the 'first among the Lord's lowly and poor', the 'valiant woman' who has known poverty and suffering, flight and exile, situations which can scarcely escape the notice of those who seek to endorse and further, in the spirit of the gospel, the liberating energies of human beings and society . . . the figure of the Virgin most Holy, far from disappointing certain profound aspirations of men and women of our time, actually furnishes the finished, perfect model of a disciple of the Lord: labourer of the earthly and temporal city, and at the same time diligent pilgrim toward the heavenly, eternal city; promoter of the justice that liberates the oppressed and of the charity that succours the needy, but above all active witness of the love that builds Christ in hearts.

The far-reaching implications of this insight not only for theological reflection on political liberation, but for a Christian feminism, will be evident, though there is no room to explore either here. Equally evident is the radical difference between Pope Paul's use of the metaphor of pilgrimage, and that of Marian piety of the hymns I looked at earlier. Here the image leads towards, not away from, engagement with and commitment to practical attempts to order the 'earthly and temporal city'. A Mariology which pursued these insights would not end, as the earlier Mariology often did, in a despairing abandonment of the temporal order in favour of a pietistic quietism or, perhaps more commonly, in the endorsement of authoritarian 'solutions' to the disorders of a world conceived as hopelessly sunk in sin and unbelief.

5

What Do We Want from the Saints?

'What's a saint?' ask the demons in Newman's *Dream of Gerontius*, and provide their own jaundiced answer:

> One whose breath
> Doth the air taint
> before his death:
> a bundle of bones
> which fools adore,
> Ha! Ha!

The demons' answer will hardly do, but their question is not so straightforward as it might seem at first sight. Take up any dictionary of the saints, and the thing that strikes you is the impossibility of generalization about the people it deals with. Notions of sanctity have changed a great deal in the course of 2,000 years of Christian history, and the long gallery of men and women who were often very much God's awkward squad defies general categories. What has George the dragon-killer got to do with Gerard Majella?

In any attempt to answer that question we encounter a fundamental ambivalence in the cult of the saints. The official Church – by which of course I mean its clerical intelligentsia and administrators – has increasingly seen the saint as *exemplar*, one who embodies some aspect of the Christian ideal, as religious teacher, figure of heroic virtue, or friend of the unfortunate. And it is not hard to think of saints who embody one or other aspect of heroic virtue – the saint as very good man or woman. Everyone's list will be different, and one can simply invoke names almost at random: Bishop Hugh of Lincoln tending lepers with his own hands or wading into anti-Semitic riots to rescue the unfortunate victims; Cardinal Robert Bellarmine in the sumptuous heart of renaissance Rome living on bread and garlic and stripping his rooms of their hangings to clothe the beggars at his door; Maximilian Kolbe offering himself as a substitute in the starvation cells of a concentration camp for a man with a wife and family. Here saint and hero merge, and in many of the saints courage and sheer sanctified bloody-mindedness are hard to distinguish – Becket, defiant in his cathedral; the 40 legionaries of Sebaste freezing to death on the ice within sight of fire and food, rather than offer incense to the emperor; Richard Gwynn, a sixteenth-century recusant schoolmaster forced in shackles to a 'heretical' Anglican service, and rattling his chains to drown the preacher's impieties.

This is sanctity for all seasons: it is not difficult to see the claims of such people to a place in the collective Christian memory, but they by no means constitute a majority of the canonized.

Perhaps the saint as dead clergyman comes nearest to a general category, for the majority of the canonized, even in modern canonizations, have been priests, bishops, or at least monks and, less often, nuns. Their lives and deeds, usually nowadays of dispiriting propriety, must pass rigorous scrutiny. But it has not always been so. In the days when popular religion really was popular religion, a saint, it has been said, was someone whose life had been insufficiently researched. A staggering number of the figures who have evoked the most passionate veneration and the most elaborate and popular of cults have in fact been entirely fictitious, or at least no more than a name round which legend has congealed. These include some of the most celebrated figures in the calendar, whose images and legends have inspired countless great works of art: Agatha, Barbara, Catherine of Alexandria, Crispin, Christopher, George – the list seems endless.

Why were they venerated? The answer seems to be that they were valued chiefly as wonder-workers, often in direct ratio to the improbability of their exploits, the saint valued as magical defender against the evils of existence – Anthony to recover lost property, Barbara to stave off sudden death, Blaise to cure infected throats, and so on. 'Look on St Christopher' runs a sixteenth-century inscription on a church wall at Finisterre, 'and go on your way assured'. The saint as thaumaturge, or visionary, or spectacular ascetic, was believed to link ordinary men and women with the supernatural, in a way unconnected with morality or even, in some cases, theological orthodoxy.

The most popular saints in late medieval England included a bizarre group of Roman virgin-martyrs – Agnes, Agatha, Lucy, Catherine, Cecilia, Dorothy: the list stretches on – whose legends were essentially cloned from and interchangeable with each other. Each of these saints was said to have been betrothed to Christ in chastity, each was pressured by parents to sleep with or marry influential pagans, usually the local Roman governor, each defiantly refused and each was sexually tortured, usually by having her breasts sliced, ripped or burned off. At the moment of death, Christ spoke to each, promising that anyone who venerated the memory of the saint would be preserved from disasters of a specified sort – they would not miscarry in childbirth, their houses would not burn down, they would never suffer death by drowning, they would not die without the last sacraments. And so their images and stories were portrayed everywhere one looked in late medieval churches, houses, on furniture, jewellery, in the popular literature people read or listened to for entertainment. This was the very stuff of the cult of the saints.

The anarchic and sub-Christian potential of this folk-religion is obvious, and its dangers have not been lost on the clerical leadership of the Church, who have accordingly exercised an ever-tighter and more centralized control over the process of canonization and veneration. The revision of the Roman Calendar by Pope Paul VI in 1969 was a case in point. Out went Benedict Labre, the eighteenth-century Italian folk-hero and simpleton who would not harm even the lice who fed on him; out went Catherine Labouré, originator of the immensely popular cult of the Miraculous Medal; out went St Catherine of Alexandria and her exploding wheel; out went St George and his dragon. [Though the wind of change did not necessarily blow everything away. The bishop of a northern see told me recently of a visit to the relevant Vatican department to secure relics. To tease the poker-faced friar in charge, he asked for a series of ever more improbable British saints: the friar was not stumped, for it seemed that specimens of all were available. At last the bishop asked, did they have a relic of St George? The custodian consulted an inventory: '*Si, si*', he replied, '*anche il dragone*' ('Yes, indeed, and also the dragon!')].

On the face of it, such reforms were decidedly in the spirit of the Council, the cleansing of an area of Catholic practice into which sub-Christian elements had crept. But the matter is not so simple. The modern emphasis on the saints as exemplars and models of the Christian life, the aspect of the cult of the saints most favoured by authority, has severe limitations. It is perpetually in danger of pelagianism, a wearisome emphasis on good deeds and moral effort, the saint as prig and puritan, which is the antithesis of much that has proved most vital in the celebration of the saints in the Christian past. The saint as prodigy, miracle-worker, protector, intercessor, has deeper roots in the New Testament than might at first appear, for there the emphasis on the holy dead was not on their good deeds, but their place in the worship of heaven as living symbols of endurance, and of the cosmic triumph of the power of God over the forces of evil – chaos, cruelty and death. The improbable choirs of tortured virgins which so captured the medieval imagination would have looked not the least bit out of place in the Book of Revelation, and served much the same purpose. These saints and their bizarre legends provided a concrete assurance that the end-times had already begun, and that the power of God, let loose in the death and resurrection of Jesus, was indeed alive and working in the world to heal and protect, to defy the forces that diminished the lives of ordinary men and women.

This sense of the eruption of the Kingdom of God into the present material world order was part and parcel of the cult of relics, which is still such a feature of mediterranean Catholicism. Mummified horrors lie above or below high altars, like St Ubaldus of Gubbio, in a glass coffin in the church high above the town whose protector he still is, which he saved from Frederic Barbarossa. Serried ranks of ormolu or tinsel-mounted skulls and bones grin out at you from their gimcrack aquariums in sacristy and relic chapels the length and breadth of Spain and Italy. These are a perpetual witness against the temptation to over-spiritualize Christianity.

Centralized control of the process of canonization has also militated against another dimension of the cult of the saints: its power to sustain and symbolize community. From the beginning this has been a vital element in the veneration of the saints. In the world of late antiquity, so powerful was the pull of the saints that bishops removed the relics of the martyrs from the rural or suburban cemeteries and shrines round which Christians increasingly gathered, and lodged their bones securely under the episcopal altar, in part at least to prevent the formation of rival focuses of the community's self-awareness. The presence of the body of the saint within the community acted as a bonding agent. Their relics became the focus of festivals in which the whole community shared, and were carried out into the streets and fields to bless them or to avert disaster. The rhythm of the sanctoral calendar differentiated one town or region from another, brought visitors from far off to the community, and was a source of pride and prestige.

To some extent the saints still serve this function – St Januarius at Naples, St Patrick perhaps, though more for the Irish in exile than for the Irish at home. But modern saints are less localized, their relics and their festivals less central to their cults. Mass-produced images, or the writings of the saints, have made their cult portable, and have therefore cut it free from its roots in particular times and places. Millions have read the Little Flower's *Diary of a Soul* who could not tell you when Therese's feast-day was, and who will never make their way to Lisieux.

This, of course, is part of the decentring of modern life in general. Few of us now live our whole lives in one place, or function to the year's rhythm, for central heating, electric lighting and winter package holidays to the sun have emptied our lives of the presence of the seasons. The atomizing of our social life means that there are fewer and fewer occasions on which everyone takes time off simultaneously, and the saints are disappearing even from the liturgical calendar, with the reduction of the number of feast-days celebrated as days of obligation. And those which remain are regularly moved to the nearest Sunday.

It is difficult to see what is to be done about this, without a revolutionary reversal of the larger social trends which are homogenizing all our lives, from Cornwall to California, as we eat the same foods, wear the same clothing styles, watch the same TV programmes. But at least we should try to nourish our awareness of the local and the particular in the cult of the saints, and be sensitive to their value as counter-cultural exemplars, living proof that small is beautiful.

So maybe we should devise ways to tell the stories of the Christian lives of those in whom we see the grace of God at work. Maybe we should also try to reinstate some aspects at least of popular canonization, by praying publicly to those of our own dead whom we believe have died in grace. There is less difference between the cult of the Holy Souls and the cult of the saints than our Western practice and some of the grimmer versions of the doctrine of purgatory have led us to believe.

All this, of course, is another reason for wishing that there was more local control over who is venerated as a saint. A communal dimension does remain in the process of canonization, but it is a debased and in some cases a dangerous one. To make a saint costs a great deal of money, effort and time. This is one reason why so few lay men or women get canonized, for they have no interest-group behind them to mount, fund and sustain their cause. It is a different matter with religious orders and similar groups, however, who can provide all these things. The canonization of the founder of Opus Dei is the most striking example in recent times of the successful promotion of a cause by a pressure group, in order to legitimize and extend the objectives of that group: here the saint becomes a mascot and a means to an end for the group who venerate him.

This political dimension of canonization is nothing new, of course – many of the Anglo-Saxon royal saints were promoted in order to enhance the prestige of the royal families from which they came, or the monasteries which they founded or in which they were buried. Henry VII and Henry VIII promoted the cause of the hapless St Henry VI in order to discredit Richard III, who was supposed to have murdered him. But the stranglehold of the papacy on the process of saint-making has made the spontaneous formation of local cults more difficult and more suspect. It is, of course, a dimension of the liturgical imperialism by which the Roman Rite eclipsed and suppressed local rites and calendars: maybe it will be reversed with the re-emergence of greater liturgical diversity.

I am encouraged in all this by a story which suggests that there is some resilience left, even in the industrial West, in the popular, if not the local, dimension of the cult of the saints. Everyone knows that St Christopher is the patron saint of travellers. He has had this role since the early Middle Ages, when he was numbered among the 'Fourteen Holy Helpers'. Not a single historical fact about him is known, and he may well never have existed. His cult dwindled after the Reformation, but revived spectacularly in the twentieth century, with the arrival of motor-travel. A friend whose word I sometimes trust swears he has seen in the USA an electronic St Christopher which can be plugged into a car dashboard: when the speedometer goes ten miles above the legal limit the statue lights up and says 'OK bud, you're on your own'. A church has been built in Christopher's honour as patron of motorists near the Citroen factory in the Javel area of Paris.

In 1969 Pope Paul VI attempted to suppress the cult of this dubious saint. There was an immediate and violent reaction all over the world, led in Italy by a group of film stars. The cult flourishes in the teeth of ecclesiastical disapproval, and the

makers of St Christopher medals and car mascots bloom and
flourish. Popular religion is alive and well and living near the
Citroen factory in the Javel area of Paris.

But in any case, what do we want from the saints? The
answer, I suppose, must be a variety of things, not always
obviously compatible. We want from them, for example, both a
sense of familiarity and a sense of Otherness, of possibilities both
within and beyond the range of our own lives. Julian of
Norwich observed of St John of Beverley that he was 'a kind
neighbour, and someone we know'. That is a recurrent theme
in the cult of the saints, and remains one of their greatest values
for us, for they help to domesticate the holy, to enable us to
grasp that it is accessible to us. To be Christlike doesn't mean
being less, but more like ourselves: more human, not more
angelic. The saints are people like us, and remain our friends,
supporting and sustaining us from the other side of death. And
so the great medieval collection of saints' lives, *The Golden
Legend*, talks of the cult of the saints as paying the 'debt of inter-
changing neighbourhood', and tells us that in venerating the
saints 'we venerate ourselves'.

But the saints are also, importantly, beyond us, visible signs of
a call to transcend the ordinariness of our own lives, and
evidence of the possibility of heroism and wonder. Nowadays
the Church minimizes the miraculous dimensions of sanctity. In
some causes, like those of St Thomas More and St John Fisher,
the candidates for sainthood were let off their practicals
altogether, the requirement of two miracles being waived. But
the recurrent presence of the miraculous in the legends of the
saints is not so easily set aside: we need some way of articulating
the deep Christian sense of the explosive reality of the divine,
the God of surprises who can shake our lives open and take us
well beyond any expectation of our own, and for whom no
situation is ultimately desperate or beyond redemption.

Previous generations of Christians were better than we are at
story-making to enshrine this perception, but we too need to
find some equivalent for this aspect of the cult of the saints if we

are to retain the confidence in God such stories expressed and nourished.

Above all, maybe, we need the saints to help us to celebrate the infinite resourcefulness and variety of the grace that has been made flesh and dwells amongst us. If in celebrating the saints we celebrate ourselves, this in the end is because in them we celebrate our truest self, we celebrate Christ. The grace that was fully present in him is endlessly at play in human beings. The humanity of God is not exhausted in the human story and personality of Jesus, but through him reaches out to fill the whole of humanity. The Protestant reformers worried that the celebration of the saints diminished the work of God, and believed that the saints were the rivals of Jesus. The opposite is the case: the saints are the expression of our deep conviction of the inexhaustible greatness and the accessibility to all of that was achieved in Christ:

> I say more: the just man . . .
> Acts in God's eye what in God's eye he is –
> Christ. For Christ plays in ten thousand places,
> Lovely in limbs, and lovely in eyes not his,
> To the Father, through the features of men's faces.
>
> (Gerard Manley Hopkins, 'As kingfishers catch fire')

6

Discerning the Body

Thirty years ago Catholics asked to identify one absolute and unchanging element in their faith might well have pointed to the Eucharist, a sacrament celebrated in what appeared to many to be the timeless splendour of an immemorial ritual, canonized in the 'Tridentine' missal but far older in its fundamentals. Catholic sacramentalism, Catholic insistence on the incarnational reality of God's presence in the world, found eloquent expression here, and actions and words converged to articulate a faith at once unchanging, ineffably otherworldly and startlingly concrete. The Catholic Modernist George Tyrrel thought that Catholic sacramentalism, above all Catholic belief and practice about the Eucharist, was the fullest and most complete translation possible of the apocalyptic Messianism of the first Christian generation, and of Jesus himself.

We might still want to point to the Mass as the fundamental encapsulation of our faith, but just what we would be pointing to may seem less immediately obvious. We now grasp, as was not sufficiently grasped before the Council, that nothing whatever in this sublunary world is 'timeless', that the Mass itself is a cultural construct, whose external rituals – music, dress, posture, language, the space in which it is enacted – encode particular understandings of Christian teaching and practice. There is of course a sense in which the folk mass, complete with improvized or paraphrased prayers, hessian vestments, lay conductors and liturgical animators, and a massed orchestra of guitars, synthesizers, and combs and paper, is the 'same' as a

Tridentine High Mass offered at an eastward-facing gothic or Baroque altar, to the accompaniment of plainsong and polyphony. Equally clearly, the two celebrations encapsulate profoundly divergent and, in some cases, contradictory sets of beliefs about the meaning and value of the Eucharist itself. And herein lies one of the most acute problems confronting modern Catholicism. Before the Council, much of our identity as Catholics was invested in the notion of a single, uniform eucharistic faith, embodied in a uniform eucharistic ritual, imposed and policed from Rome. Where and what is that identity now, given the diversity of Catholic eucharistic practice and, therefore, belief?

The diversity of belief is an observable fact. Watch any queue for Communion, in any sizeable congregation, in any Catholic church in the English-speaking world. Watch, in particular, the teenagers and children, who will approach the altar, hands by their sides or even in pockets, who will take the Host often between thumb and finger from the priest's thumb and finger, like a biscuit, and on returning to their places will slump in their seats or gaze about them as if they have just come back from the bathroom. No doubt I exaggerate, but the essentials of this picture will be familiar to any regular churchgoer, as will be the general boredom and inattention of many children during the eucharistic prayer and the words of institution. It seems to me patently clear that this behaviour is quite simply incompatible with the sort of beliefs about the nature of the eucharistic species and the mode of Christ's presence in the Mass with which Catholics were brought up before the Council, and I therefore deduce that these young people do not hold those beliefs.

My point here is not to do an elderly impersonation of 'Disgusted of Tunbridge Wells', but to point to a theological and pastoral problem. We need to be clear that you cannot have the 'same' faith as before, while engaged in radically different liturgical behaviour. If sacramentalism means anything, it means that we embody what we believe, and explain it to ourselves, in gesture, so that if the gestures diverge, so also will the beliefs behind them. This is not to argue that we should keep or revive all the old gestures, for that would be to try to canonize one moment of human culture over all others, to 'freeze' a particular set of liturgical gestures in an attempt to fix the beliefs behind them. There is no firm standing in the shift and flux of time. What we can do is try to see the old liturgy more clearly as a cultural construct, to discern what values informed it, then to ask ourselves which of those values as Catholic Christians we need to retain, and to work out ways of doing so in our cultural situation. *(True of Protestant also.)*

If one had to single out one dominant element in Catholic eucharistic behaviour before the Council, it might be to point to eucharistic *realism*. It was hammered home to us that the eucharistic Host (we were not greatly interested in the contents of the chalice) simply *was* Christ – body, blood, soul and divinity. First-Communion cards showed the Divine Child relaxing in the tabernacle, or a ghostly and wounded Christ transparently hovering over the ciborium. The rituals surrounding the handling, reception and reservation of the Host emphasized this ultra-realism. The priest kept his thumbs and first fingers pressed together between the words of consecration and the ablutions, in case a microscopic fragment of the precious Body was trapped there. I can remember still the mixed horror and delight of my first Communion class when a De La Salle brother told us that if a communicant was sick, the regurgitated Host was to be rescued from the mess and consumed, provided the priest was able to do so without nausea!

This tremendous insistence on the absolute reality of the eucharistic Presence emerged decisively in Latin Christianity about the year 1000 partially in response to eucharistic controversy, and greatly increased as a consequence of the new and more precise formulations of the great age of scholasticism in the twelfth and thirteenth centuries. Earlier ages of the Church had of course believed in the Real Presence, had recognized in the Eucharist the central sacrament, but had been more conscious of the figurative dimension of sacramentality, and less keen to define, to itemize. Even St Augustine, that fountain-head of so much that was most characteristic of the Catholic theology of the Middle Ages, cautioned against overprecision about the Eucharist. 'If you ask how this can be so', he wrote, 'I will tell you briefly. A mystery of faith can be profitably believed: it cannot properly be examined.' But increasingly theologians wanted to examine it, to penetrate the mystery, and devotional and liturgical writers tried to nail down in prayer and gesture a new sense of the concreteness of the Presence.

At times this realism seemed to threaten the very nature of the sacrament, which both is and is not, which delivers reality but points beyond itself to a greater, fuller reality. At the beginning of the eleventh century Cardinal Humbert could write that 'I believe that the bread and wine which are laid on the altar are, after the consecration, not only a sacrament but also the true body and blood of our Lord Jesus Christ, and they are physically taken up and broken in the hands of the priest and crushed by the teeth of the faithful, not only sacramentally, but in truth.' Aquinas and the Dominican tradition would be more careful about the notion that Christ himself was moved, lifted, broken when the sacred species were so treated, but the whole drive of Western eucharistic practice was to embody just such an understanding. The Host ceased to be recognizable bread, and became a paper-thin wafer which need not, and indeed should not, be chewed. Made from a wheaten paste of a degree of refinement found in no other bread, it was baked between hot iron moulds coated with wax, no longer made by bakers but by clerics ritually dressed in surplices. The purity, whiteness, roundness of the Host became the mirror of the spiritual reality it concealed. The sacrament was no longer understood as the transfiguration of an ordinary thing by the Divine Life, but the presence in a sullied world of an object of transcendent purity and unworldliness, whose appearance and handling should reflect this. Ordinariness did not enter into it. The Host became something ineffably other, transcendentally distant.

That transformation was reflected in eucharistic devotion. Central to Christian understanding of the Eucharist was the knowledge that the Eucharist made the Church, that it constituted the Body of the Lord in the communal as well as the more narrow eucharistic sense. 'It is you yourselves that are laid upon the altar', Augustine had written, 'it is to your own mystery that you say "Amen".' One consequence of the new emphasis on the literal reality of Christ's presence in the Host was a loss of this wider understanding of the nature of Christ's body, and a growing sense of distance between the communicant and the Holy Thing he or she received. Eucharistic prayers emphasized the purity of the Host, the vileness of the recipient – sin against holiness, darkness against light, foulness and fountains.

All this, of course, had abundant scriptural and patristic precedent: what was new was the skewing of emphasis one way to the exclusion of other perceptions. One result was that lay people, already nervous of approaching the sacrament, became more so: lay communion by the central Middle Ages was a rarity. Eucharistic sharing, communion, ceased for most people to involve consuming the Host, and became instead a matter of *seeing* it. The introduction of the elevation of the Host in Mass was connected to controversy about the doctrine of 'concomitance' – whether or not the whole Christ was fully present in either species – hence the decision to insist that he was, by raising the bread, alone for adoration immediately after the words of consecration over the Host. This elevation became the centre of lay religious piety. The Body of the Lord was out there to be gazed upon, as objectively concrete as the vessels that contained it. The Host began to be reserved in crystal containers so as to remain visible, in sacrament towers with grilles or windows to allow adoration, a trend which culminated in the institution and spread of the feast of Corpus Christi, which arrived in England in the early fourteenth century.

The effect of all this was to place the reality and the presence of God *outside* the Christian, to objectify it, in a classical movement of alienation. The positive side of this was to draw out the sense of the majesty, otherness and holiness of God, of the transience of this world, of the incompleteness of human life, and its necessary orientation towards the Kingdom.

Tyrrell's linking of the sacraments and early Christian eschatology exactly catches the strengths of this type of eucharistic piety. Its weakness was precisely that of alienation, of making the Christian people feel that the presence of God was something other than and far beyond them. I remember once hearing the comedian Spike Milligan tell an interviewer that, though a Catholic, he never went to Communion, because *it* was too good and *he* was too filthy.

This objectification of the presence had even uglier consequences. If the Body of Christ could be identified literally and simply with the Host, then the enemies of Christ were of course also the enemies of the Host. It was a recurrent medieval fantasy that Jews and heretics secretly practised ritual desecration of the Host. Jews in particular became the target of countless libels, in which they were alleged to have stolen or bought consecrated Hosts in order to recrucify or otherwise desecrate them. These stories usually involved miraculous refutations of their impiety, in which the Host bled copiously, or was transformed into gobbets of bloody flesh, or burned or choked the blasphemers. The stories were often used as the pretext for the persecution and even execution of Jews, and relics of such miraculous desecrated Hosts – or of the sacred blood alleged to have flowed from them – became common. Anyone who has visited the beautiful chapel of the Miracle of Bolsena in the cathedral at Orvieto can see some of these anti-Semitic stories portrayed in the frescoes to the left of the altar and in the vaulting above. Response to the Host had become the touchstone for identifying hated outsiders.

In tracing these developments, of course, I am selecting a single strand in medieval eucharistic belief and practice. The great merit of the medieval Church's eucharistic understanding was its richness and diversity. The very texts and liturgies which encapsulated the trends I have been discussing witnessed to older and different emphases, and the full range of Catholic thinking about the Eucharist was there to be discovered. The growth of a new realism by no means meant that only a literal, single-level understanding of the Eucharist was now possible.

To take a single example, we may look at the famous antiphon which St Thomas Aquinas composed for Vespers on Corpus Christi. In Latin it runs *O sacrum convivium, in quo Christus sumitur, recolitur memoria passionis ejus, mens impletur gratia, et futurae gloriae nobis pignus datur, alleluia,* which roughly translated means 'O sacred banquet, in which Christ is received, the memorial of his passion celebrated, the mind filled with grace, and the pledge of future glory is given to us, alleluia'. But the words of the antiphon work at a variety of levels. *Sumitur* does not simply mean 'received' or 'eaten': it also means 'assumed' or 'put on', 'understood', 'begun', 'chosen', 'affirmed' or 'believed'. Eucharistic eating therefore for Thomas means here not just a literal eating, but the process of opting for Christ, believing in him, assuming or putting on his life, understanding his teaching and beginning discipleship. A similar richness of meaning can be found in the word *pignus*, which is not just a pledge, but a symbol or sign, a first instalment or down payment of a future reward, a lover's token. The richness of reference in medieval liturgical language here prevents a narrowly realist interpretation squeezing out other dimensions of the Church's eucharistic understanding.

In the wake of Vatican II, the realist theology which dominated Catholic eucharistic thinking for nine centuries was not challenged or abandoned, but it was in many ways quietly replaced with a different theology and a different starting-place. If the older liturgy and devotional practice had highlighted the objective presence localized in the Host, the new liturgy emphasized the communal dimension of the Lord's body. The recovery of that sense of communal involvement as the Body of Christ, and the growth of universal lay communion, has been a tremendous success: at its best the modern liturgy witnesses to a sense of comprehensiveness and involvement which is quite new to the Latin tradition, though central to New Testament and patristic teaching.

But there has been a price. In a quest for freedom from neurosis and pettifogging ritualism, a whole gamut of practices which seemed to many at the time unnecessary or even super-

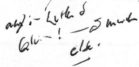

stitious was dropped or formally abolished – the eucharistic fast; the restrictions on the handling of the vessels used in the Mass; ritual practices like the holding together of the priest's fingers after the consecration. The shape, size, texture and colour of the Host changed, too: it became something to be chewed, sometimes indeed it seemed to be made of muesli and glue, and fewer and fewer people thought it sensible to worry about the crumbs that might be generated by consecrated Hosts. Communion in the hand and the widespread use of lay people as 'Extraordinary ministers of the Eucharist' lessened the sense of fear and awe, the sense of *noli me tangere* which surrounded the Host. In many parishes the service of Benediction became a rarity, or was altogether abandoned, as priests wedded to a newly discovered understanding of the Eucharist as *food*, became increasingly unenthusiastic about the theology which underlay eucharistic adoration in this particular form. With the abandonment of this world of gesture, the theological beliefs and emphases which they enshrined began to lose their grip on the minds of Catholics, especially those with no memory of the older pattern.

It could of course be argued perfectly sensibly that there is nothing to lament or regret here. No age can fully grasp all the riches of Catholic belief about the Eucharist. The age that ended with the Council was strong on the reality of Christ's presence in the eucharistic elements, but weak on the communal dimension of that presence, which is just as real and just as important. We have recovered that vital reality, and if we are less able to express or realize other aspects of the Eucharist, we should not worry unduly.

It seems to me that this line of argument will not do. The problem with modern eucharistic piety is that in expressing a sense of the presence of Christ in the community, it constantly teeters into Pelagianism, a comfortable sense of the simple continuum between human and divine community. The painful and contradictory reality of our unity in Christ despite our class and racial antagonisms, our divergent interests, our fears and mutual suspicions, the sheer brokenness of human society, is buried under a cosier sense of the niceness of all being together. The Church of Vatican I is often accused of identifying the Church with the Kingdom, but that is an accusation which cuts very near the bone in the Church of Vatican II, where our understanding of what is going on at the Eucharist often does just that. We need to be reminded that the Kingdom has indeed been given, but as a *pignus*, a pledge of something still not within our grasp, still 'out there'. The majesty and glory of the risen Christ belongs to us, but is not yet our possession. It is still something before which, if we do not quite take off our shoes, at least we must take our hands out of our pockets. The holy presence of our God challenges as well as informs our efforts at community, and we still need the prophet's sense that we are men and women of unclean lips, and dwell among a people of unclean lips. The Host is a burning coal to cleanse, as well as a morsel to nourish.

And so we need to keep alive that objectifying realism of the older tradition, alongside our own discovery that we not only adore, but *are* the Body of Christ. Where the older tradition encapsulated within itself a variety of levels of meaning, modern liturgy tends to opt for a single meaning, to offer prose in place of the older poetry. We have allowed the vocabulary of gestures used in the Eucharist to become thin and single-level, good at expressing our sense of a realized unity in the Body of Christ, less capable of capturing the beauty and otherness of God, the mystery of the gift of himself which he forges out of our ordinariness into something new and strange.

It is time we began once again to look for ways to express that threatened but vital dimension of Catholicism. We need to kneel more, maybe once again to fast from ordinary foods before we eat the food of angels, to learn to handle the Holy Thing as if it were something other than cream crackers, to recall our wandering attention to the central moment of the great prayer in which the mundane is gathered up into the eternal. The old props, lights and bells and incense, can still be used in ways which are not mere frills, to underline and sober us into a sense of just what a treasure it is that we casually take for granted. We need to make more space in the garrulous bustle of the modern Mass for reflection on and gratitude for the mystery of God's self-giving, which is, now and always, the still point of the turning world.

But has the lord's supper in the early church much more like ideal?

7

Why Do We Need the Pope?

I see that some publishing firm has recently published a set of books carrying the title 'The Sex Lives of . . .' The first two volumes in the series deal with *The Sex Lives of the American Presidents* and (yes, you've guessed it) *The Sex Lives of the Popes.* This is old hat, of course. No doubt the book will have plenty to say about Alessandro Borgia, baptizing his own illegitimate children and keeping a nubile young mistress in the Vatican. But the annals of papal Rome would yield a rich crop of scandal for anyone intent on digging it out. For every papal saint, one can find a papal sinner, not only during the Renaissance period, in which colourful villains or worldly princes like Alexander VI, Julius II and Leo X flourished, but maybe even more in the ninth and tenth centuries, when the papacy was in the pockets of the warring Roman baronial families. The Church in that era was treated to a succession of popes of the calibre of Benedict IX, a brutal thug elected when not much more than a teenager, and himself the nephew of two popes. Benedict was utterly cynical and a bad pope even by the standards of the day – he was deposed by the Roman crowds, hardened as they were to fairly dreadful bishops. He had himself forcibly restored, with much bloodshed, but ultimately resigned, having sold the papacy to his godfather, Gregory VI, for a thousand pounds, it was rumoured because he needed the money to get married.

Stories like this – and there is no shortage of them – used to be grist to the mill for no-popery pamphleteers, but it is probably salutary for Catholics to bear them in mind from time

to time. Since the nineteenth century the papacy has been
surrounded with a superhuman mystique and an aura of sanctity
which has rather obscured from us the real nature of Catholic
belief about the place of the papacy in the Church. We have
idealized the popes, dehumanizing them and turning them into
holy icons or superstars, and have then projected onto them
unreal dreams and expectations.

And of course the popes have often co-operated with this
process, for they, like other Catholics, have shared the popular
glamour which surrounds the papal office. And no wonder.
The papacy is, after all, the oldest, and certainly one of the most
influential, of all human institutions. The Roman Empire was
scarcely born when the first popes sat in the seat of Peter. When
Karol Wojtyla became the 263rd pope in 1978, the dynasty he
represented had outlived not merely the Roman and Byzantine
empires, but those of Carolingian Gaul, medieval Germany,
Spain, Britain, and the Third Reich of Hitler. In the years that
followed, John Paul II himself was to play a significant role in
the collapse of the latest of these empires, the Soviet Union.

But for Catholics, of course, there is more to it than an awe-
inspiring pedigree. Over the centuries, and especially in the last
150 years, the papacy has become the spiritual centre of the
Church, directly appointing all but a handful of the world's
bishops, exercising a watching brief over all the affairs of the
churches, a mixture of policeman and nanny in everything that
concerns the life and belief of Catholics. We tend to take all this
for granted, and, if asked to account for it, most Catholics
would probably end up quoting Matthew 16:18 – 'Thou art
Peter and upon this Rock I will build my Church' – as if it
explained everything. We believe that Christ gave to Peter a
special ministry and the first place among the apostles, and that
it is the Lord's will that that ministry should be continued
within the Church by the bishops of Rome. What is not always
grasped is just how differently that Petrine ministry has been
understood and exercised in the history of the Church.

In the earliest and most formative centuries of the Church, it
was hardly a reality at all. Until the time of Leo the Great, for

example, the popes played very little part in the formation of
the fundamental Trinitarian and Christological beliefs of the
Catholic Church, for these were mostly hammered out in the
East. In the so-called Dark Ages the papacy became the spiritual
centre of the Christian West, but that cut no ice in the East, and
even in Western Europe it did not involve the sort of hands-on
control of the Church that we take for granted these days.
Bishops were appointed, saints canonized, local councils
convened, liturgies composed, all without papal involvement.
The great reforming popes of the eleventh and twelfth centuries
struggled, not to gain the appointment of bishops for
themselves, but to make sure that bishops were properly elected
by the local churches, and not by local kings. Even the most
commonly used title of the modern popes, Vicar of Christ, was
almost unheard of for the first twelve centuries. All bishops,
kings and emperors were thought of as Vicars of Christ: what
marked out the pope was that he was Vicar of St Peter, the
apostle's living mouthpiece and earthly representative.

What has been, may be again. It is conceivable that the
Church of the future might be less centralized, that bishops
might once again be really chosen by the local churches, or that
local canonizations might be celebrated without reference to
the Congregation of Rites. Yet even if these things were to be
so, there would still be a Petrine ministry, and the papacy would
remain God's will and God's gift to the Church. In the flux of
time, then, just what is it that lies at the heart of the papal office?

One tempting answer might be that what we mostly value
about the papacy is the infallibility of its teaching. But this seems
to me clearly to put the cart before the horse, for to claim that
would be to identify the uniqueness of the papacy with what is
least characteristic and distinctive about it. The infallibility we
believe papal teaching to possess in certain circumstances is in
fact, as the definition of 1870 carefully states, a particular
exercise of the same infallibility which Christ willed for his
whole Church. Besides which, papal infallibility is what the
word itself suggests, a fall-back, a fail-safe device, the Spirit's
guarantee that, when the chips are down, the Church will not

be allowed to fall away from the truth. But the charism of infallibility (if one may talk about it as a charism, which I suspect to
be misleading) has been exercised extremely rarely, and it
would surely be absurd to identify the primary value of the
papacy with so unusual an activity – rather as if we were to
define the function of a fire brigade as rescuing kittens out of
trees.

And in any case, the definition of infallibility tells us nothing
at all, of course, about the routine teaching of popes and other
bishops, when the survival or integrity of the faith itself is not at
stake. Like their fellow bishops, popes can be clever or stupid,
effective or inept, alert or lazy, well or badly advised, and they
can be all or any of these things in their teaching as in any other
aspect of their ministry. There are good popes and bad popes,
popes who are great theologians (like Leo I or Benedict XIV),
and popes who are lousy theologians (like John XXII or
St Pius X).

What remains, then? What is it about the papacy that as
Catholics we cannot do without? It is, surely, in the first place,
its apostolicity. The pope is for us what Peter was for the first
Christian community: in being so, he focuses for us a larger
truth about the episcopate and the Church as a whole. In a
concrete, particular, fallible and sinful community, as once
among the motley company of the apostles, about most of
whom we know nothing more than their names, the pope is a
sign that the truth of God is to be found and will not fail.

We need to be clear just what is and is not involved in 'apostolicity'. The apostles were and are, first and foremost, witnesses
to the mighty works of God. The Church is built on them, not
because they were spiritual geniuses or inspired leaders, but
because in the providence of God they happened to be there
when God sent his Son to be the Saviour of the world. Their
value to us lies precisely in their ordinariness and their weakness
– in the fact that they were men, as W. H. Auden wrote:

> Without arms or charm of culture,
> Persons of no importance

> from an unimportant province
> They did as the Spirit bid,
> Went forth into a joyless world
> Of swords and rhetoric
> To bring it joy.

Lacking both force and rhetoric, the message of the apostles is that of simple witness to what they know to be the truth. Peter was their leader, but that does not mean he was the cleverest, the bravest or the best. The great theological genius of early Christianity was Paul, not Peter, and the disciple most beloved by Christ was John, who lay upon his breast in the night he was betrayed. The Peter of the Gospels and Acts is warm hearted, eager, but a blusterer who, at the crisis of his life, lacked the courage of his convictions and denied his Lord. This was the Rock on which Christ chose to found his Church.

Early in its history the Church was confronted by subtle, brilliant new teaching which took the simple message of the first Christians and tried to adapt it to the sophisticated religious ethos of the Hellenic world of the second century. The result was what we call 'gnosticism', religion for the elite of a new age, the wisdom of the *cognoscenti*, the sophisticated. The Church fought it with ordinariness, making the acid test of Christian belonging not expertise in religious theory or knowledge of secret teaching, but simple sharing in the Church's public worship, obedient attention to her scriptures, and communion with her bishops, the administrators who had emerged as successors of the apostles, handing on their teaching, preaching that old-time religion. The bishops became the public sign that God had tabernacled among real people, that the eternal had entered not into secrecy and the glamour of the arcane, but into the mundane, the public and the ordinary.

It was shocking teaching, and men and women have always found it so. The successors of the apostles, the foundation stones of the Church, could be cowards, like Peter − they might run away in persecution, or worse, stay and betray the truth by handing over the scriptures or revealing the names of their flocks. During the era of persecution, the fallibility and ordinariness of the bishops who did this, the scandal of apostolicity, led some purists to break away from the unity of the Church in the search for something above and beyond fallibility, looking for leaders who were holy, and therefore could be believed. That sort of idealism, which is ultimately a failure of faith in the Incarnation, has dogged the history of Christianity ever since. The episcopate, and in a special way the papacy, are a God-given witness against it. The apostolic witness of the Church, focused in her bishops, is a witness that the saving truth of God has been handed on to sinful men and women like ourselves. It is not to be found by walking away from the community of sinners we call the Church – according to St Augustine, a hospital for incurables – to lonely places, higher morality and secret teaching. Instead, it is only to be found in the unity of a shared and faltering pilgrimage alongside other sinners, relying not on superior resources but on the truth of God released among us and proclaimed whenever Christians meet to hear the scriptures and break the bread of life together. The episcopate – and especially the papacy – embody the sheer flesh-and-blood uncompromising humdrumness of redemption, the particularity of God's presence in his world and in his Church,

That is why Catholics symbolize their unity in Christ around a person – the bishop, the pope – rather than basing it on a theology – Calvinism, Lutheranism. Of course we have to assume that bishops and popes are men of faith, hope and charity, and we have to hope that they will live up as well as they can to the demands of the gospel and the trust we place in them, that they will be very wise and specially holy. But they sometimes don't and aren't, and in the end that isn't what matters most. We stick with them not because they are clever or nice, but because they are the ministers of God, and to whom else shall we go? To be a Catholic, at times, is to feel like the man in the rhyme:

> Beware of letting go of nurse,
> For fear of finding something worse.

And that is why we do no service to the gospel by pretending that our bishops or popes are superhuman, that they never commit sins or make mistakes. This is the special error of a particular sort of papalism, which imprisons the reality of apostolicity by refusing to see the pope as a man like other men, with likes and dislikes, prejudices and presuppositions, virtues and vices, all of which shape, for good or ill, his actions and his policies. Gregory VII even believed preposterously that all popes were automatically made saints by the merits of St Peter (an utterance which posterity has not deemed to be infallible!). Modern Ultramontanism has often implied much the same thing, if not quite in the same terms. We are all guilty of this to some extent, we all want the pope to be a hero, a genius, a saint, a star.

The papacy, then, is a witness to the ordinary, the mundane. It is the external sign of our inescapable involvement with each other, of the fact that God calls us not into some future invisible Church, but to the responsibilities of a real community, which will support and nourish us, but which will also make demands on us, demands which may not always seem reasonable or right. The leadership of bishops and popes is, of course, a God-given means of grace: the gifts and talents of the men who hold the office, in all its particularity, are part of God's providence for his Church. But even in the Church, maybe especially in the Church, there is, as they say, no such thing as a free lunch. If the particular experience and outlook of popes and bishops are one of the ways in which God graces the Church, they can also be one of the trials of the Church. The saints and giants, the great succession of popes who nursed whole churches and civilizations into being, are part of the story – Leo I, Gregory I, Innocent III, Innocent XI, John XXIII, John Paul II. But so also are the villains, the disasters, the weaklings – Stephen VI, Alexander VI, Clement XIV. And life being what it is, good and holy men have been disastrous popes, like Celestine V, and great popes have helped shape appalling events, like Urban II who launched the Crusades, or Pope Leo IX, one of the greatest reforming popes of the Middle Ages, yet who played a key and catastrophic role in the hardening of the tragic schism between the Eastern and Western Churches. Nothing and no one can write the papacy out of the history of the Church and the world, but to construct a balance sheet of benefit and damage wrought by the popes involves a commitment of faith as much as an assessment of fact.

Yet no one can doubt the centrality of the papacy in the unity of Catholicism. That unity has often been, and can still seem, an enforced one, a conformism of style informed by timidity and enforced by thought-police, the suppression of legitimate variety within the Church. The history of the Eastern Catholic Churches, whose customs and independence were for centuries devalued and eroded by Latinization, is evidence of that possibility. But who can seriously doubt the fundamental role of the papacy in holding together in a single communion churches with vastly different histories, priorities and cultures – the churches of Europe and Africa, of the First and the Third Worlds, churches, moreover, often separated by national and ethnic confrontation or conflict of interests. It is the papacy which more than any other element holds all the churches to a common vision, and helps prevent them collapsing back into the parochialism of their own regional or cultural agendas. Because we must all live with the papacy, we are all enabled to live with each other.

The extraordinary personality and formidable talents of Pope John Paul II bring some of these considerations into sharp focus. He is an Ultramontane, a man filled with a profound sense of the immensity of his own office, of his centrality in the providence of God. He is convinced, for example, that the shot with which Mehmet Ali Agca almost killed him in 1981 was miraculously deflected by Our Lady of Fatima; and when, a few years ago, like many another old man, he fell in the shower and broke his thigh, he interpreted the accident as a deeper entry into his prophetic calling: the pope, he declared, must suffer.

Suffering, one may feel, is the key to his character: the death of his mother when he was nine, of his beloved elder brother when he was 13, the harshness of his wartime experience as a

labourer in a quarry and in a chemical factory, the years of concealment, resistance and confrontation as seminarian, priest and
bishop under Nazi and then Communist rule. All these have
shaped an outlook half grieved by and half contemptuous of the
self-indulgence of the West, dismissive of the moral and social
values of the Enlightenment which, he believes, have led
humanity into a spiritual cul-de-sac and have more than half
seduced the churches.

He is a hard man to measure. Sternly authoritarian, he is
nevertheless a passionate believer in religious liberty, and at
Vatican II played a key role in the transformation of Catholic
teaching in that area. Often seen as dismissive of other faiths, he
has initiated acts of worship involving Hindus, Muslims, the
Dalai Lama and assorted Shamans: when praying at the scene of
Gandhi's cremation he became so absorbed that his entourage
lost patience and literally shook him back into his schedule. The
uncompromising defender of profoundly unpopular teaching
on matters such as birth control, he is nevertheless the most
populist pope in history, the veteran of over 60 international
tours, an unstoppable hand-shaker, granny-blesser, baby-kisser.
Convinced of his own immediate authority over and responsibility for every Catholic in the world, he has gone to the
people, showing himself, asserting his authority, coaxing,
scolding, joking, weeping and trailing exhausted local hierarchies in his wake.

The titanic energy of this pontificate has had momentous
consequences for the Church. Not all have been good. The
endless journeys, designed to unite the Church around the
pope, have sometimes seemed rather to highlight divisions.
The rhetoric of shared responsibility with other bishops has
often been belied by increasing Vatican intervention in the local
churches, not least in some disastrous and disastrously unpopular
episcopal appointments. In all this, one can see the reversal
of trends inaugurated by his predecessors, like the devolution of
authority to local churches which was so striking a feature of
Paul VI's pontificate.

John Paul II is the very embodiment of a particular and very exalted vision of papacy, and so he is a figure of contradiction as well as of unity. He has been hailed by some as God's reply to the Second Vatican Council, and denounced by others as an oppressor of women. The unpopularity which his stance on a host of issues has brought him, troubles him not a whit. In the solemn and silent moment of his episcopal ordination in Poland, a former workmate from the chemical plant shouted out the Pope's nickname. 'Lolek,' he cried, 'don't let anyone get you down.' For good or ill, he never has.

And whatever one's view of him, his pontificate is certainly a sign that the papacy still has work to do, a momentous role to play in the history of Church and world. It surely seems more than a coincidence that a Slav pope, and such a Slav, should have been in office at one of the great crises of world history, the collapse of the Soviet bloc. Those who are ill at ease with his style can hardly doubt his impact, or his power for good. To my shame, I remember grumbling bad-temperedly about the media hype surrounding his visit to England in 1983. A non-Catholic colleague listened silently to what I had to say, then remarked, 'I daresay all that is true: I'm just glad to know that there is a good man in a white robe standing up for decency and truth.' It is not a bad summary of what the papacy means, or can mean, for everyone.

8

Papal Authority

What is papal authority, what ought it to be? As the author of a general history of the papacy in 150,000 words, I suppose I ought to have a ready answer to both questions. The forced march through 2,000 years of Christian history which the research and writing for that book involved, however, left me with at least as many questions as answers; above all, with a sense of the intractable complexity of the historical reality of the Church and its institutions.

Catholics tend to assume that the development of the papacy has been a steady evolution from Christ's appointment of Peter as the one who would 'feed my lambs' to John Paul II's world tours and solemn pronouncements on the objectivity of morals or the non-ordainability of women. Most people are vaguely aware that papal authority as we know it was not exercised by the early popes, but the later powers of the popes are assumed by Catholics to have been implicit in the more limited authority the early popes did actually possess. History, alas, is not so simple: the development of the papacy is not in any straightforward sense a matter of the steady unfolding of implicit powers and functions. Authority is never a matter of paper theory or mere status: it is embodied in real powers, and takes its meaning from the exercise of those powers. Yet many of the most characteristic functions of the papacy, like the appointment of bishops, are very recent indeed, and originated less in any scriptural or patristic basis than in the vagaries of history, and in the confusion of roles which were in theory quite distinct.

From the earliest times, of course, the Church of Rome and its bishops had a special place in the churches of the Mediterranean world, and especially in the West. In practice, however, that primacy was experienced, and understood, quite differently in different regions. In most of peninsular Italy, the pope was in effect the sole archbishop, and his power, like that of other archbishops, was wide ranging and very direct. The popes called and presided at synods, ordained the bishops, intervened to regulate discipline and enforce the canons. Outside Italy, in the West more widely, this metropolitan authority only obtained directly in those areas where the popes had succeeded in establishing and maintaining vicariates, a succession of local episcopal representatives through whom they exercised supervision – at Arles in Gaul, in the Balkan regions, and briefly for Spain at Seville under Pope Simplicius (468–83). These Apostolic Vicars were thought of as sharing the papal 'care for all the churches', and they were given the pallium as a sign of their co-operation in the papal ministry.

Elsewhere, the pope's authority was that of the patriarch of the West, on a par with that of the patriarchs of Alexandria, Antioch, Constantinople and Jerusalem, over their regions, though the pope's patriarchal authority was uniquely enhanced by the added prestige of Peter's authority. That prestige, however, was a matter of moral authority rather than of administrative power. It was occasional rather than constant, for the regional churches governed themselves, elected their own bishops without reference to Rome, held their own synods, ordered their own life and worship. Rome was important not as a daily presence, but as a fundamental resource, the only apostolic see in the West, above all functioning as a court of appeal in special circumstances. This last function was to be crucial in the emergence of papal theory: the 'case law' built up in the course of such appeals was formalized in the corpus of canon law, and helped shape Western thought about the Church, and the central place of the papacy in it.

For the churches of Gaul, Africa and Spain, then, the characteristic expression of papal primacy was not a matter of executive rule from Rome, which they would certainly have rejected. Instead, the Petrine ministry was experienced in the form of occasional interventions, almost always in response to local requests, designed to give the added solemnity of apostolic authority to the decisions and actions of the local churches.

In the East it was yet another matter. There the papal primacy of honour, derived from the succession to Peter, was indeed acknowledged, but the practical consequences the popes deduced from it were ignored or denied outright. Rome was seen as the senior patriarchate, one of five, the *Pentarchy*, whose harmony and agreement were the fundamental apostolic under-pinning of the Church's authority. In Eastern thought, for example, the recognition of a council by the Pentarchy came to be seen as the decisive mark of a 'general' council, whereas, in the West, recognition by the pope alone was the crucial criterion. Above all, the claim of Constantinople, the new seat of the Empire, to be 'New Rome' in religious as well as in secular terms, was a constant threat to papal primacy, which the popes actively tried to counteract; in the end, unsuccessfully.

There were then three distinct functions within the early papacy: metropolitan, involving a direct, 'hands-on' role in the local churches of Italy; patriarchal, involving a looser and more reactive responsibility as point of reference and court of appeal for the West more generally; and the 'Petrine' or primatial ministry, a much less clearly defined place of honour among all the churches, East and West, whose precise implications were never universally agreed, and which were looked on with con-siderable reservations in the East. Much of the history of the papacy has been the collapsing of these three distinct roles into each other, and the growing claims of the popes to exercise all three functions as if they all involved metropolitan authority everywhere – as if the promises to Peter made the popes, in effect, archbishops of every province.

That convergence – some would say confusion – of the papacy's three functions can be clearly seen in the extraordinary growth in papal power, and papal intervention, in the churches of the West from the mid-eleventh and twelfth centuries. Rome had originally been conceived as the court of final appeal: in the course of the twelfth century it took on the role of a court of first instance. The pope became the 'universal ordinary', exercising direct jurisdiction in every corner of Christendom, dispensing judgements which were built into the precedent books and became the basis of law. The roots of this development were religious, based in the traditional Roman interpretation of the commission of Peter. As St Bernard of Clairvaux wrote to Pope Eugenius III:

> It is true there are other doorkeepers of heaven and shepherds of flocks: but you are more glorious than all of these . . . they have flocks assigned to them, one to each: to you all are assigned, a single flock to a single shepherd . . . You are called to the fullness of power. The power of others is bound by definite limits; yours extends even over those who have received power over others.

For Bernard as for Gregory the Great this lofty commission was a call 'not to dominion, but to ministry through the office of your episcopacy'. Yet Bernard had no doubt that this ministry demanded that the pope be exalted. 'Why should you not be placed on high, where you can see everything, you who have been appointed watchman over all?' It was the work of the medieval papacy to transform this religious perception into legal reality. Canon law became one of the principal fields of intellectual effort and advance in the Middle Ages, and the codification of law put the papacy at the heart of the Church, as the monarch and his courts lay at the heart of secular legal systems.

All this had a negative side, which was much commented on. The right of any cleric to appeal to Rome, and the prohibition of local action against him while the appeal was pending, meant that culprits could fend off just punishment almost indefinitely by appealing to the pope. The judgements given in the papal court on cases far away was often based on insufficient information, or the one-sided presentation of a party in a dispute.

Ecclesiastical superiors could be harassed by mischievous accusations against them at the papal court. Bernard of Clairvaux
would warn Eugenius III against undermining the hierarchy of
the Church – 'You have been appointed to preserve for each
the grades and orders of honours, not to prejudice them.'

The medieval papacy also hugely expanded its rights in the
appointment of clergy and bishops. Bishops had been locally
elected in the early Church, and in the early Middle Ages they
had just as often been appointed by kings and princes as by any
other method. What went for bishops went twice as emphatically for lower offices, but in the later Middle Ages the
papacy gradually captured more and more of these appointments for itself by reserving the right to 'provide' or appoint to
all benefices whose incumbents died while they were in Rome.
This prerogative was steadily extended, and the papal court
gradually became responsible for the appointment of huge
numbers of clergy. Papal provisions benefited more people than
the pope. Fortune-hunters all over the Church besieged the
Curia with requests for preferment through the papal
machinery, not least the crowned heads of Europe, who
discovered that the cheapest way of paying their great servants
of state (mostly clerics) was by securing bishoprics and abbeys
for them by means of papal provisions. None of this was implicit
in Christ's promises to Peter, none of this had been dreamed of
by the popes of the early centuries, yet the idea that the pope
was directly 'in charge' drew at least as much substance from the
contingent fact of his ability to appoint men to jobs all over
Europe, as from any theological consideration.

Papal rights of appointment to benefices and bishoprics
fluctuated wildly. The late Middle Ages were its high point, but
from the Renaissance onwards the growth of the nation state,
and the jealousy of secular rulers over outside interference,
changed all this. Steadily, the pope was forced to concede more
and more appointments, especially of bishops, to the secular
ruler. In 1753 the best pope of the eighteenth century, Benedict
XIV, conceded to the king of Spain the right to appoint to
12,000 benefices in Spain, leaving the pope with just 52. The

move almost bankrupted the hoteliers and inn-keepers of Rome, for within a matter of weeks 4,000 Spanish job-hunters left Rome and stampeded back to the Spanish court to jockey for promotion.

This process of whittling down papal control went on until the mid-nineteenth century, as the popes bargained with the monarchies of Europe and beyond to secure freedom for the Church's work. The breakdown of social order in the French Revolution taught the rulers of Europe that they could not rule without the help of the Church: bishops and priests were needed to preach obedience and contentment. Bishops and priests cost money, however, and because the Church had lost its endowments in the Revolution, it needed state funding to pay its ministers. The state valued the clergy, but demanded the right to appoint the men it paid, and Rome had no choice but to agree, even when the governments were Protestant (as in Prussia). By 1829, 555 of the 646 diocesan bishops of the Roman Catholic Church were appointed by the state. Another 67, in the USA, Ireland, parts of Germany, Belgium and Switzerland were locally elected by cathedral chapters or some similar arrangement. The pope, acting as sovereign of the papal states not as bishop of Rome, appointed 70 bishops. As pope, he appointed directly just 24 in Russia, Greece and Albania.

This massive transfer of episcopal appointments to the state had of course been well under way before the French Revolution, but the Revolution altered the terms on which it was taking place. In the high Middle Ages the papacy had struggled to destroy the system of 'proprietary churches', by which laymen had appointed bishops. The theological motive of the popes was to secure the Church's freedom in appointing its pastors. It did not identify that freedom with itself, and since the Second Lateran Council (1139) the 'normal' method of episcopal appointment had not been papal nomination, but real election by the local church, in the form of the cathedral chapter. For financial reasons, the later medieval papacy, especially at Avignon, had slowly eroded this situation to capture more and more episcopal nominations for itself.

Theoretically, however, capitular election remained normative, and from 1814 until the 1860s, wherever the popes were free to do so, they preferred capitular election to other methods of appointment. But many cathedral chapters had been swept away by the Revolution after 1789, and where they were restored, the Concordats often ignored or removed their electoral powers. In effect, the Concordats, and state payment of bishops, recreated the proprietary system by which secular rulers paid the bishops, and therefore demanded the right to choose them.

Ironically, it was the steady secularizing of Europe which led to a change in papal responsibility in this matter. Secular rulers, anxious to distance themselves from the Church, ceased to want to appoint bishops. The most spectacular shift came in Italy. In November 1870 Italy, formed in part out of the confiscated papal states, passed the Law of Guarantees, to regulate relations between Church and state. As part of the law, the state surrendered any claim to the appointment of bishops. In theory, the pope refused to recognize this law. In practice, however, he tacitly adopted many of the provisions as a working arrangement, allowing clergy to accept the revenues of their benefices from the state, and himself taking over the appointment of all Italian bishops. This was a move of enormous significance. Italy had a greater concentration of bishoprics than any other part of Christendom, and as new territories were annexed to the kingdom, Victor Emmanuel had accumulated immense powers of appointment, greater than those of any other king in Christian history. By 1870 he had the right to appoint 237 bishops. All these appointments now came into papal hands; and not only transformed the relationship of the pope to the Italian episcopate, but shifted expectation about the papacy's role in episcopal appointments generally.

From now on, there was a growing but quite new assumption that the pope was the right person to appoint all bishops. Paradoxically, the loss of the temporal power of the popes enormously increased papal control not only over the Italian Church, but over the Latin Church more generally. The change took place when Western theology of the local church was weak, when the freedom of the Church over against the state was imagined almost exclusively in terms of papal freedoms. So it is no surprise that the new expectation that the pope would normally appoint all bishops was enshrined in the new code of canon law promulgated in 1917. The overall effect of the code was a massive increase of centralization. It owed more to the spirit of the Napoleonic Code than to scripture or patristic tradition (scripture is rarely quoted in it), and it canonized as permanent features of church life aspects of the papal office which were very recent developments. In particular, canon 329 declared that all bishops were to be nominated by the Roman pontiff, setting the seal of legal time-lessness on a radical extension of papal responsibility which had taken place virtually in living memory.

None of these developments were inevitable, none of them were implicit in the scriptural promises to Peter or the earliest Christian reflection on the Petrine office. This means that much of what we consider most characteristic of the modern Petrine office has accrued to the popes through the merging of distinct functions, and through the vicissitudes of quite recent history. And what comes by historical accident may go by historical accident. The present powers of the popes in such matters as episcopal appointments are open to assessment on grounds of utility, efficiency and theological fitness, and might be changed on any one or all of these counts. It is not obvious that the choice of a bishop for Brisbane, Borneo or Birmingham is best decided in Rome, nor that the wishes of the local churches and their bishops should be ignored when it comes to such choices – as they often are.

In the past, the grandeur of papal claims has been moderated by the brute realities of rival powers. The most exalted prerog-atives of the popes often rang hollow because they were impossible to put into force. The pope might claim to be universal ordinary, but the existence of rival legal systems, con-flicting rights, the claims of powerful secular rulers, even the sheer length of time correspondence took to get from one place to another moderated those claims, created a system of checks and balances. This was especially so in the Baroque period, when the pinnacle of papal power was symbolized in the sublime vulgarities of the Baldacchino in St Peter's or Bernini's collonade, but when papal influence over the Church was in fact being increasingly marginalized by the great powers. Cardinal Richelieu, ruler of France, declared of the pope that 'We must kiss his feet, and bind his hands.' Yet the grandiose claims of the popes in the age of the absolute monarchs, however hollow, did help to prevent the churches of Europe becoming imprisoned in national agendas, and kept alive the concept of a universal Church which meant more than a mere chaplaincy to universal empire. Without the papacy, Europe might have invented Stalinism three centuries early.

In a world in which the state has essentially given up interest in the Church, and in which e-mail, the fax, the telephone and the jet plane have eliminated distance, the checks and balances have gone, there is no one to bind the pope's hands. For the first time, the Church has a papacy whose power is almost equal to its claims. This is certainly dangerous for the local life of the churches, and will have to be addressed in the new millennium. As every papacy draws to its close, it is a favourite party-game among Catholics to imagine their dream pope. A recurrent scenario is the pope who will surrender his supremacy, restore the papal primacy to its primitive role of support and honour, a *papa angelicus* who will bury the sceptre of power and use only the force of persuasion and good example. It will not happen, of course, and on the whole it should not happen, for any sudden transformation would be likely to be catastrophic. The Church in the USA, for example, is deeply divided, increasingly polarized between right and left, prey to a babel of conflicting caucuses and sectional interests. Many American Catholics, especially those with feminist convictions, view the papacy with undisguised suspicion and even hostility. No doubt papal interventions in the USA have helped foment as well as control these divisions, but it is equally obvious that the papacy is currently the strongest glue holding the centrifugal energies of American Catholicism in some sort of unity. If the pope were tomorrow to surrender his role in the choice of American bishops to local processes, the result would be likely to be schism: it might also remove one of the barriers against the drastic surrender of the American Church to cultural, moral and economic values which sit very uneasily indeed with the demands of the gospel.

The papacy in its present form is the work of history and circumstance, as well as of divine intention. The disabling paternalism and interventionism which is current Vatican style (and has been 'current' for centuries) are not the inevitable development of the promises to Peter, but the work of time and circumstance. Yet if the papacy has developed its claims to a level dangerous for other forces and freedoms within the Church, it is also one of the Church's most precious and irreplaceable assets. History is tangled, messy, contradictory. But is where we are.

9

Who Leads the Church?

Who leads the Catholic Church? The tempting, obvious and, in an important sense, the *wrong* answer is the pope, of course. Catholic thinking about leadership is often dogged, even bedevilled, by the fact of hierarchy. We are an hierarchical institution: no account of the Church could be considered Catholic that did not have somewhere close to the centre the notion of order, ordination, the grades of ministry, the centrality of the episcopate, above all, of the bishop of Rome (though perhaps I should not have written here, 'above all', because this sort of metaphor of vertical space, the notion of 'above' and 'below', smuggles into our discussion right at the start emphases which are liable to skew our thinking). The bishop is at the heart of the local church, the pope is at the heart of the universal Church.

And if at the heart, we say, then at the head. The bishops are our leaders, the pope in a special sense is our leader. And there is a school of thought – usually called Ultramontanism – which takes it as an axiom that since he is our leader, we must always obey the pope. Loyalty and obedience are concepts often invoked in association with church discipline or teaching, as if it were a flag to which we ought to rally. My country right or wrong, my Holy Father, wise or foolish. It is worth reflecting, I think, on just how odd that conclusion is, because the relationship between obedience and leadership is by no means uncomplicated. There are, of course, leaders who expect, and have a right, always to be obeyed – obvious examples might be a general on a battlefield, or a surgeon in an operating theatre.

You cannot have soldiers debating the wisdom of their orders in the face of the enemy; you cannot have three different people arguing the toss about whether or how an artery had better be tied up. But these are crisis models, and hard cases make bad law.

We are familiar with the extension of military models of leadership into other areas of life, and the application of the rules which govern the very atypical society of an army, to the ordering of society at large. We call this phenomenon Fascism, and it has nothing at all to be said for it as a model for the Church. By contrast, we have many examples of leadership – that of the head of a research team, or a schoolteacher, for example – where leadership is exercised not by issuing commands, but by suggestion, provocation, challenge, and where space for the led to propose alternatives and even make mistakes is an accepted part of the process.

In practice, the pope's leadership is a curious amalgam of roles. In the first place it is sacred and symbolic, it is sacramental: the pope is the only person prayed for by name at every Catholic Eucharist, and is therefore quite evidently a special focus of our eucharistic unity. The invisible and spiritual unity of the cacophonous hotch-potch of peoples, races and tongues which make up the universal Church finds its visible focus in the unity of every Catholic with their bishop, and of every bishop with this one bishop.

The symbol is of course not empty, not *merely* ritual. The unity of heart and head symbolized by episcopal communion is cashed in the faithfulness of the local churches to the apostolic tradition to which the pope is the chief witness. In practice, this will sometimes mean that local preferences or convictions have rightly to be set aside or modified in deference to the pope and the tradition of which he is the custodian and ultimate spokesman. And this much has been true of the papal office as far back as records of its functioning take us. A papal primacy which was *merely* symbolic, which did not in the end involve a willingness on our part to accept a concrete judgement, to defer to the tradition made specific, not just as a general notion, but in particular courses of action, would be empty and of no practical service to the Church.

But in the second place, the popes in modern times have functioned in a rather different and more proactive mode, as managing directors of a multinational company, ensuring brand uniformity in all the local branches, hiring and firing middle management, dictating the nature and availability of the company product. Leadership as management is a very recent aspect of papal leadership indeed, and though it has a long pedigree in papal claims and papal theory, as a phenomenon in the real world there is nothing specially venerable or sacrosanct about it.

Its dominance as the normative mode of papal interaction with the local churches is largely the result of relatively recent historical happenstance – the emergence of globalizing forms of government and administration in the wake of the French Revolution; bulldozing away local particularities and exemptions; the invention of rapid communications such as the railways and the telegraph (and nowadays the Internet); the collapse of the monarchies of the ancient regime, who had so jealously contested with the papacy their immemorial claims to appoint bishops and regulate their Churches. Their demise, and the secularization of the states of Europe that followed, left a vacuum which the papacy filled.

There is a case, of course, for considering all this as providential, and one may well feel it is better to have the pope appoint the bishops than Benito Mussolini or General Franco, or even Tony Blair, but it would be hard to argue that forms of papal government that took the best part of two millennia to emerge were of the essence of the institution itself. Unless one really does believe that the Holy Spirit comes out of the barrel of a gun, it is dangerous to make too close an identification between what happens in history and the will of God.

And about the exercise of papal leadership in this more proactive sense, there is a good deal of obfuscation. In the first place, we identify with the papal office many functions which a moment's consideration will make clear are actually or ought to be, wholly or partly, located elsewhere. Consider here, for example, the notion of the *magisterium*, leadership as teaching. In theory, the ordinary *magisterium* of the Church is exercised by every bishop (and shared indeed by many who are not bishops, from theologians and parish clergy down to the mother teaching a child to say the Lord's Prayer). In practice, it is closely identified with papal utterances. I once spent some months living and teaching in Rome, an experience which was for the most part profoundly inspiring and exhilarating. Less inspiring, and in the end dispiriting, was my discovery of one of the fundamental facts of life in Rome; namely, that all Roman church officials, no matter what their theological opinions or stance in ecclesiastical politics, no matter what the occasion, endlessly quote the reigning pope. Every address from every cardinal, bishop or Vatican functionary will be larded with snippets of the wit and wisdom of John Paul II, the printed version solemnly adorned with marginal references to encyclicals, apostolic exhortations, allocutions, Angelus addresses.

This is, of course, part of the etiquette of a particular sort of court, and though it is depressing to have structural toadying of this kind built into the routine business of the Church's central machinery, it is I suppose understandable. More seriously, however, it underlines a dangerous theological error, the notion that the pope is the principal source of teaching and theological expertise in the Church, and that everything he says or writes is double-distilled wisdom, and worth repeating. This is a mischievous opinion on several counts. First, because it foolishly and idolatrously exalts the intellect of the men who get made bishops of Rome to a stature by no means all of them warrant; and second, because most of what the pope says or publishes is actually written by somebody else and, these days particularly, sometimes vetted only very cursorily by the pope before he delivers it. This is obviously the case with the minor papal speeches prepared for the pope's many travels, but it is also true of most papal encyclicals, which, over the two centuries for which they have been the most authoritative form of papal utterance, have usually been ghostwritten.

Of course the issuing of an encyclical by a pope makes the utterance in some sense his own, no matter who actually wrote it, but the fiction of his authorship should alert us to the fact that, whatever has been the case in the pontificate of John Paul II, particularly in its early years, most of the hard thinking in the Church goes on elsewhere than in Rome, and papal theology is rarely at the cutting edge of authentically Catholic thought. When we list the great teachers of the Church over two millennia, only a handful of popes qualify, and in the nineteenth and twentieth centuries the popes were more often the leaders of theological parties than the founders of schools of thought. The twentieth-century pope who most prided himself as a teacher was Eugenio Pacelli, Pius XII, and he did indeed issue momentous and influential encyclicals; but essentially even the best of them recycled other people's thoughts, none of them would stand up as ground-breaking exercises in constructive theology, and the truly great Catholic teachers of his era, de Lubac, Congar, Rahner, the Fathers of the Council, all fell under suspicion or suspension while he reigned.

None of this is to disparage or deny the fundamental importance of the papacy in the process of Catholic teaching, merely to emphasize that the pope's role has historically been that of an anchor, not a pioneer or trail-blazer. We should tremble at the thought of a radical pope and, thankfully, there have been very few. Inventive leadership, the sort of originality of spirit or intellect which leads to breakthrough or a rank shift in the way Christians view the gospel and the world, rarely comes from the Church's officers, but is usually the result of a charism, which indeed an individual bishop or pope may possess as a God-given grace, but as a Christian individual and not by virtue of his office. So the intellectual leaders of the nineteenth-century Church were not the popes of that era, but social and political theorists like De Maistre and Lamennais, preachers like Rosmini, or theologians like Moehler and Newman, none of whom were bishops; nor, as that list suggests, were they by any means all leading in the same direction, or to equally beneficial effect.

These distinctions are perhaps easier to see in the Church of the past than the Church of the present, so it is worth considering for a moment the character of Christian leadership at the pinnacle of the so-called Ages of Faith, the start of the thirteenth century. All the ambiguities of leadership, and the delicate balance between office and charism were in evidence during the pontificate of the most remarkable pope of the Middle Ages, Innocent III (1198–216). Innocent was a devout and intelligent Paris-trained theologian and Bologna-trained lawyer. Author – while still a cardinal – of a banal but best-selling devotional treatise which survives in more than 700 manuscripts, he was elected pope when he was only 37 years old. From the outset of his pontificate he tackled the problems of the Church with gargantuan energy, and no one had a higher understanding of papal leadership than he had. It was Innocent who made the title 'Vicar of Christ' current as a description of the pope, and he believed himself to be, like the prophets of Israel, set above nations, greater than men but less than God, with authority over every aspect of human life. Convinced that secular rulers held their mandate from God only so long as they ruled for the benefit of the Church, he excommunicated and deposed the German Emperor Otto IV. He also placed England under interdict and excommunicated King John for refusing to accept the papal consecration of Stephen Langton as Archbishop of Canterbury. Later, when John had submitted and made his kingdoms a feudal fief of the papacy, Innocent was equally ferocious in the now tamed king's defence, embarrassingly declaring the attempted curb on royal power we call Magna Carta to be null and void.

But most of Innocent's energy was directed into more recognizably religious channels. The papacy of the high Middle Ages needed to coax, as well as compel, kings and bishops to throw their weight behind the programme of reform and renewal which had underlain papal strategy for the Church since the eleventh century – the renewal of monasticism, the celibacy of the parish clergy, the eradication of bribery and simony, the

instruction of the laity in the fundamentals of the faith and its
regular practice.

To achieve episcopal solidarity behind papal reform, the
popes harnessed the machinery of 'General Councils' (though
they were in practice Councils of the Western Church only).
Innocent himself presided over and masterminded the proceedings of the greatest council of the Middle Ages, Lateran IV,
convened in 1215, at which transubstantiation was defined, the
obligation of the bishops to provide Christian teaching at every
level emphasized, and the obligation of the faithful to receive
the sacraments of penance and Eucharist at least once a year was
first imposed. Lateran IV created the framework of Christian
practice and instruction which was to shape and define Latin
Christianity for the rest of the second millennium, and the
pope's energy and vision accounted for a large part of its
programme and its success.

But his pontificate also had less happy results: Lateran IV
solemnly endorsed the notion of Crusade against Islam and
against Christian heretics, and it was Innocent III who first
blessed and legitimated the use of force against the Cathar
heretics of southern France, the so-called Albigensian Crusade:
that precedent was to unleash a tidal wave of blood in the
centuries ahead.

Innocent can stand, therefore, for institutional leadership at
its best, encouraging lay participation, education and instruction, promoting pastoral reform, the papacy at the heart of the
Church stirring others to responsible action. Equally, his
leadership inaugurated or confirmed less happy trends, the use
of imprisonment and slaughter to defend the gospel, the claims
of the Church to authority in secular affairs. And the Church of
his day was full of individuals and of movements profoundly
uneasy with this whole style of leadership.

As the papacy exalted itself and the institutional Church grew
richer and more powerful, there were many who looked for the
recovery of the gospel in a return to simpler values, radical
poverty and the repudiation of worldly power. Many of these
movements tipped over into heresy, denying altogether the

authority of the hierarchy, the value of the material world, and the engagement of the Church with the secular order. Despite his authoritarian understanding of the papacy and his horror of heresy, Innocent was remarkably sensitive to the positive value of such prophetic witnesses within the Church, and made strenuous efforts to retain such movements within the bounds of orthodox Catholicism.

His most spectacular success here was his legitimation of the early Franciscan movement. Francesco Bernardone and his first followers were radical laymen, whose refusal of involvement in the money economy and identification with the poorest of the poor might easily have led them into the wilderness in which other such movements had fizzled out or turned world-denying or revolutionary. When Francis sought papal approval for his followers' way of life, Innocent shrewdly annexed them to the Roman Church by tonsuring them (thus bringing them under episcopal control as members of the clergy) and giving them verbal permission (he hedged his bets by writing nothing down) to preach and exhort on matters of morals and Christian practice. Though Lateran IV subsequently forbade the founding of new religious orders, the Franciscans were able to plead this verbal approval by Innocent III as a warrant for their new rule. The movement rapidly became the fastest-growing and most important spiritual phenomenon of the Middle Ages, and its mainstream would remain ardently loyal to the papacy. Francis was in a sense the mirror image of Innocent III, an inspired and inspiring leader who repudiated altogether money and secular authority, and whose hold over his followers owed nothing to his office (he surrendered formal leadership of the movement to others) but was entirely due to his personality and charism. All the early Franciscans were groupies, won for the movement by the electric personality of its founder.

In the same years, Innocent recognized another radically new movement which would help to transform Latin Christianity. To combat the theological arguments of the Cathar heresy, he authorized the preaching of a group of priest-preachers led by the Spaniard Dominic Guzman. From this little group, who established themselves at Toulouse, would emerge the Dominican Order, the most important intellectual force in the late medieval Church, and which in Thomas Aquinas would produce the greatest Christian theologian since St Augustine. The vision behind the Dominican order was utterly different from either the hierarchic and authoritarian model embodied by Pope Innocent, or the personality cult centred on Francis. Dominic was self-effacing (we know little or nothing about him because his followers wrote down almost none of the vivid anecdotes and character sketches which dominate early Franciscan literature). His order was astonishingly democratic, the brethren taking corporate decisions, their structures of authority designed to minimize the domination of individuals, and instead to focus and facilitate their shared vocation as preachers, teachers and students of the gospel, a democracy of the intellect harnessed to the propagation of the faith.

In Pope Innocent, Francis and Dominic, are embodied the three major forms of Christian leadership – institutional, charismatic, intellectual; or, to put it in other terms, structure, spirit, theology – the kingly, the priestly and the prophetic dimensions. The Church needs structure and order if it is to survive; it needs fire, ardour, heart, if it is not to become a prison for the spirit; it needs intellectual rigour and commitment to the truth if it is to have a gospel to preach. A Church in which one or the other of these elements dominated or was unchallenged by the others would be intolerable – rule-bound, or in retreat from ordinary life, or with no truth to proclaim. Innocent III was the unquestioned head of the Church over which he presided, and both Francis and Dominic sought papal approval for their movements. But the papacy was the means of anchoring those movements within the Church, not their initiator or inspirer: the spiritual and intellectual leadership of the Church in the age of Innocent III lay in Assisi, Toulouse, and in the University of Paris, not in Rome.

The backward glance has a good deal to tell us about the nature of leadership in the Church of our times. The Ultramontane Church placed far too much weight – and far too heavy a burden – on hierarchical leadership, imagining (or pretending) that bishops and popes contained in themselves all the requirements of Christian leadership – institutional and organizational, spiritual and intellectual. In fact, hierarchical leadership is rarely initiative-taking, and its most solemn responsibility is not the setting of agendas for the Church of its time, but the recognition and fostering within the community of those less predictable energies and gifts of leadership which God showers on those outside the hierarchy. Hierarchical leadership, properly exercised, is in large part about making space for non-hierarchical leadership. At a time when the Church has been presided over for a generation by a pope who is by any measure a great man in his own right, and whose intellectual and spiritual stature has been such that it is easy to confound the merits of the man with the nature of the office, these distinctions seem worth dwelling upon.

10

Rome of the Pilgrims

I was lucky enough in 2001 to spend a semester as a visiting professor at the Gregorianum, the international Jesuit University in Rome. With the job went a house on the Coelian hill, in the grounds of the Irish College. Above the garden wall yards from my door rose the squat bell-tower of the Quattro Coronatti, the extraordinary eighth-century fortress-monastery (now a convent) whose silent cloister, a cool green shade on the hottest days, is one of the most secret of all the secret places of Rome. The church and convent are tucked above and to one side of the pope's ritual route to his Cathedral, the Via San Giovanni, that extraordinary straight street which plunges down from the Lateran square to the Colosseum. This is one of Rome's tourist hot-spots, seething with camera-laden visitors at all times of the year, but even in high summer my street, the Via dei Santi Quattro, did not seem in the least like a thoroughfare to one of the world's most famous buildings in Europe's most tourist-troubled city. Instead it resembled a remote country road, overhung with self-seeded trees and for much of the day populated only by scraggy yawning cats. And from its tranquillity, week by week, I was able to get to know, slowly and on foot, an ancient city previously encountered in breathless tourist-stops. It proved an intensely moving and stirring experience. For a church historian, those months of total immersion in a city where the Christian past is visible everywhere inevitably focused reflections on the power of Rome as a holy place.

I had been to Rome many times as a tourist myself, but also as a pilgrim, most recently during the Jubilee year, when I snatched a day between lecturing commitments to make my way (I confess slightly furtively) on foot round the major basilicas, dutifully performing the pious works required to gain the Jubilee indulgence. Like most modern Catholics, I am at best ambivalent about the theology of indulgences, even in the cleaned-up form in which they are nowadays presented: but since an evangelical protestant Archbishop of Canterbury had been willing to help the Pope launch the Holy Year by opening the Holy Doors with him at St Paul's Outside the Walls the previous January, it struck me as churlish for a card-carrying Catholic to quibble at theological niceties.

And to anyone with the slightest historical sense, that pilgrim journey on foot round the great shrine churches of Rome is an overwhelming experience, however coolly Anglo-Saxon one's normal style of piety. Holy Years themselves are venerable institutions. They have been held in Rome, first at 50- and then at 25-year intervals, for seven centuries, since 1300, when the first was declared by Pope Boniface VIII. Boniface was one of the more problematic popes of the Middle Ages, accused in his lifetime of everything from megalomania to sodomy. Whether the accusations were true or false, Boniface was and is nobody's hero – in the *Divine Comedy*, the poet Dante places him head-down in hell in a furnace of molten metal. Yet Dante himself made the journey to Rome during that first Holy Year. Poets, like historians, waste nothing: there is every reason to think Dante was a pious pilgrim, but he kept his eyes open and his wits about him, and when he came to write his epic of the after-life, he modelled the traffic arrangements in the more crowded districts of Hell on those he saw in use to regulate the Holy Year crush on the narrow pilgrim thoroughfares connecting St Peter's and the rest of Rome.

But Roman pilgrimage long pre-dates the Holy Years: already by the middle of the second century pilgrims from Asia Minor were coming to pray at shrines or 'trophies' erected over the tombs of Peter and Paul: the greatest thinker of early

Christianity, Origen, made the long journey from Alexandria to
Rome *ad limina apostolorum*, to the threshold of the Apostles.
From our end of the 2,000-year history of the Church, the
shock value of that fact is dulled: Rome for us is the administrative and spiritual centre of the Church, and a natural focus of the
sacred. But one needs only flick through the pages of the Book
of Revelation to realize that for many early Christians Rome
was a hateful and idolatrous place, Babylon the great, its soil
soaked with the blood of the saints, part of a doomed demonic
conspiracy to subvert the gospel and murder its heralds.

The irony by which the heart of the pagan empire became
the chief shrine of Christendom was not lost on the early
Christians; indeed, in the generations immediately after the
Emperor Constantine's conversion the victory of Christian
Rome over Pagan Rome was a major theological theme, the
Empire itself understood by some as a miracle of providence
designed to prepare the world for the reception of the gospel.
Peter and Paul displaced Romulus and Remus as the new
founding fathers, and the Roman Church constituted its
identity round the memories not only of the two great martyr
apostles, but of the city's other martyrs from the heroic age of
persecution, the apparently defeated and murdered Christians
whose cause had now triumphed. Their shrines, at a string of
catacombs along Rome's great approach roads, and in the
cemetery basilicas, like San Sebastiano, San Lorenzo and Santa
Agnese 'outside the walls', became holy places, to which men
and women flocked for blessing and healing. The names of the
martyrs were embedded in lists recited at the heart of the Mass,
on either side of the words of consecration, the pedigree of the
Roman community, the heroic men and women whose blood
had been the seed of the Church, and who now lived, crowned
and victorious, to make intercession for the communities which
bore their names, treasured their relics, and honoured their
memories.

The tombs and memories of the martyrs remain part of the
fundamental power of 'Roma Sancta' to move and touch the
pilgrim: underneath the steely money-making tourist bustle, it is

still, for those who care to look, a city of saints. During my term in Rome I made a point of visiting as many of the shrine churches of the saints named in the canon of the Mass as I could. To walk through the afternoon heat to a church like Santa Agnese, a couple of miles out of the city on the Via Nomentana, one of Rome's busiest roads, is to cross 17 centuries in a couple of hours. Agnes was a teenage girl martyred by having her throat cut around the year 303. Her church, erected first by the Emperor Constantine less than a generation after her judicial murder, is the modest surviving remnant of a basilica once almost as large as the old St Peter's: nearby is the extraordinary circular mausoleum of Constantine's daughter, Costanza.

The church itself is partly subterranean: you approach it by a steep flight of stairs lined with early Christian and medieval tombstones carved with invocations of the saint. Above the altar is a bizarre statue of Santa Agnese, adapted by fitting a Christian head on to the torso of a pagan goddess. In the apse above, Pope Honoriuus the First commissioned a barbaric mosaic of the saint (and himself) in the seventh century. In it the little Roman girl is a dominating presence, immense in size and dressed like a Byzantine empress. The mosaic is an example of the endless overlaying of history you find everywhere in Rome: when this ancient and rather alien picture was made, the legend of Agnes was already four centuries old.

Most moving of all, in the crypt beneath the altar, behind an iron grill, is the rather dusty blackened casket in which rest what is left of the bones of the little Roman girl whose name is recalled every time the Roman Canon of the Mass is recited. To kneel there in the cramped stillness of the ancient ambulatory round the shrine is to place oneself in a succession which stretches back into the ancient world, to touch a time in which the name of Christ still had an unfamiliar ring, and to which the gospel came first as treason, and then as an immense and liberating surprise.

It is also to perform an act of solidarity with countless thousands of pilgrims over 17 centuries, who have come to this

place, and to the many other places like it in Rome, because
Rome's saints had become their saints too. Many of the
churches of the West, from the Balkans to the Celtic fringe of
the Roman world, whose customs and calendar differed in
many ways from those of Rome, nevertheless considered
themselves in some sense allied to the Roman Church, because
they used the Roman Canon of the Mass at every Eucharist.

One of the most moving snapshots of an early Christian
British pilgrimage to Rome is Bede's eye-witness account of the
departure from Anglo-Saxon Northumbria of the aged abbot
Ceolfric, driven by an overwhelming longing to lay his bones in
Rome. Ceolfric was in fact leaving what we might call a virtual
Rome for Rome in reality: the monastery he left behind him
was dedicated to St Peter, its church adorned with Roman
icons, its monastic chant modelled directly on that used in
St Peter's in Rome, the chapel in which the abbot made his final
prayers before departure consecrated to Rome's martyred
St Laurence. But the Rome he journeyed towards (he died en
route) was also a 'virtual' Rome, a city of the imagination
whose saints and ancient churches were experienced by pilgrims
as an anticipation of heaven, the living embodiment of the
heavenly city which was the goal of the Christian life. Anglo-
Saxon England had been re-Christianized from Rome, and
owed much of its ecclesiastical structure, liturgy and theology to
the popes: the loyalty of men like Ceolfric was natural enough.
But the fame of Rome's saints and its appeal as a proto-type of
the eschatological Holy City spread even beyond the reach of
the Roman liturgy. A group of seventh-century Irish monks
visiting Rome encountered in the same pilgrim hostel travellers
from Egypt, Palestine, Greece and southern Russia.

For the first thousand years of Christian history, then, the
appeal of Rome was essentially as a vast cemetery, in which
rested the bodies of famous saints, above all the two chief
apostles, Peter and Paul. But for the Christians of the first
millennium, possession of the bodies of the saints was far more
than custody of their corpses: it meant participation in their
charisms and their heavenly power. Because Rome possessed

the bones of Peter and Paul, the Roman Church was informed by the wisdom and authority of Peter and Paul. Though it was not his cathedral, St Peter's basilica became the pope's principal church precisely because it was the cemetery where the apostle lay. In the papacy's own book of annals, the *Liber Pontificalis*, the pope is often referred to simply as 'the Apostolic one', his role defined by his relationship to Peter. And so, when Charlemagne was crowned emperor in Rome by Pope Leo III on Christmas Day 800, the ceremony took place not in the cathedral at the Lateran, but in St Peter's, at the tomb of the apostle: the new Roman emperor would be the protector of the tomb of the saint whose death had conquered and redefined the glamour of the old Roman Empire.

So Rome of the pilgrims, and the tombs of Rome's saints, above all the tomb of Peter, remained fundamental to the religious authority of the papacy. As the authority of the pope established itself across the churches of the West, it came to be symbolized by the gift of the pallium to the archbishops of the churches of the Roman obedience. The pallium is a thin circular stole of white wool embroidered with black crosses. It could and can only be bestowed by the Pope. But historically it was more than the pope's livery: it was also a symbol of association with the martyrs of Rome – the wool it was woven from was blessed at the church of Sant Agnese on her feast-day, and the pallium itself was blessed by being placed overnight on the tomb of St Peter. Power and authority flowed from these holy bones. In all this the pope was secondary. Though the authority of the pope was revered in the West and respected in the East throughout most of the first millennium, nobody came to Rome primarily because the pope was there, but rather for the sake of the holy dead.

By the high Middle Ages guide-books to Rome were essentially catalogues of the city's relics, but from the fourteenth century onwards they also began to list the indulgences attached to veneration of particular relics or churches by the popes. For the religious authority of the pope was now combining with the inherent holiness of the saints in a powerful blend which reflected the growing centrality of the papacy in Western religious thought. And by the fourteenth century Rome had become central in other ways too. During the first millennium the approval of Rome was often seen as a major and even an indispensible asset for new religious ventures, such as the Anglo-Saxon mission to pagan Germany. But new ideas and new religious movements never *originated* in Rome, and by and large the local churches got on with their lives with little reference to the popes. By 1300 all that had changed. The papacy had become the centre of a vast system of canon law, and was now the court of final appeal for vast tracts of public life inside and outside the Church, playing a major role at every level of Christian life, from the granting of indulgences and dispensations to the appointment of clergy from the humblest rectories to the richest archbishopric. Rome was now not merely a vast shrine, but a vast law-court and a clearing-house for patronage and financial benefits. Inevitably, corruption and the rule of the backhander flourished. From a holy city, Rome came to be seen as a centre of sleaze: bitter Christian satirists all over Europe deplored the new situation. The only saints venerated in Rome nowadays, it was said, were Saints Albanus and Rufus, white and red, silver and gold.

In fact, soon after the Holy Year of 1300 all this business moved elsewhere: the popes, often absentee anyway, now left Rome altogether, and settled at Avignon in the south of France, where they were to stay for more than 70 years. Deprived of its living 'saint', the pope, Rome languished, its fountains and aqueducts dry, its sewage system clogged, its public buildings shabby and leaking: the Lateran cathedral itself became chronically dilapidated, its floors littered with falling tiles: pilgrimage, though it never ceased, declined. It was to rectify this situation that the great Renaissance popes began to build, daringly ripping down and replacing many of Rome's most ancient churches, most spectacularly Constantine's own basilica of St Peter's. The new St Peter's would take almost two centuries to complete, and when completed would be perceived not as a shrine for the bones of Peter so much as a throne-room for his living successor.

For in the slow evolution towards modernity in the centuries since the Renaissance, two very different forces combined to alter radically the appeal of Christian Rome. One was the revival of respect for pagan antiquity, the other was the dramatic recovery – or invention – of an extremely exalted theology of the papacy. Medieval pilgrims to Rome knew perfectly well, of course, that the city had once been the centre of the world's greatest empire: their guide books identified, sometimes correctly, the most notable of the classical buildings visible above the rubble and vegetation of centuries, and monuments like the Colosseum then as now inspired admiration and wonder. But these were the ruins of an alien past, in which there was little living interest. The Forum, once the heart of ancient Rome, was overgrown, a place of caves and rough grazing: Romans called it the *Campo Vacco*, the cow-field. What mattered most about Rome were its Christian churches, their relics and their indulgences. From the Renaissance onwards, however, travellers, especially Protestant travellers, reversed these values: Italy's ancient classical buildings replaced its Christian shrines as the focus of attention. Goethe, on his first Italian journey, deliberately hurried through Assisi by night to avoid the 'Gothick' barbarism of the Franciscan shrine and its glorious frescoes, pausing instead to admire the classical temple (sadly converted to a church) which still stands in Assisi's central square.

Gibbon would be inspired to write his monumental *Decline and Fall of the Roman Empire* by his disgust at hearing Franciscan friars sing Christian prayers in the church of Ara Coeli on the Capitol hill, where once the temple of Jove had stood. Christianity in Rome was perceived by such men not as providential victor, but as the cuckoo in the nest, ousting a noble pagan past by a tawdry Christian present. Nineteenth- and twentieth-century restoration of the historic centre of Rome would seek to peel away the Christian overlay, and the tourists would come now as much for Forum, Capitol and Circus as for St Peter's or St Paul's outside the walls.

But if this new appreciation of the pagan past threatened the ancient priorities of Christian Rome, so too did a new set of emphases within Catholicism. The nineteenth century saw the emergence of a dramatically altered type of papacy, more centralized and more personalized than ever before. Modern communications put the popes more immediately in touch with the local churches. The collapse of Christian monarchies all over Europe, and their replacement with secular states increasingly content to leave the control of religion to the pope, left the papacy the unchallenged centre of Catholicism. For the first time in Christian history, the popes appointed most bishops, and so exercised a quite new influence over the character and theologies of the local churches. The confiscation of the papal states and the end of the pope's temporal power made him instead the 'prisoner of the Vatican', the persecuted father of the world's faithful. Now pilgrims to Rome came to see the pope, to receive his blessing, to touch his hand, as much or more than to venerate the holy bones of which he had been of old essentially the guardian.

To visit Rome's ancient shrines, not least as part of a Holy Year, however, is to be offered a corrective to the cult of the leader which surrounds the modern papacy, sometimes uncomfortably reminiscent of the personality cults of the secular absolutisms of the twentieth century. Those holy bones remind us that sanctity and hierarchy are different things, that Christianity is about the life and death faithfulness of ordinary people, like little Agnes, rather than about power and authority, however sacred. The saints of Rome, whose names are part of the fabric of our most ancient and precious prayer, recited with the names of our own loved ones, living and dead, whenever the Roman Mass is celebrated, help us to grasp something of the difference between authority and tradition, and of the supremacy of tradition over authority in the hierarchy of Catholic value. Every living system needs authority – order, rule, a way of arriving at consensus and of agreeing courses of action. The papacy is Catholicism's chief and indispensable symbol of such authority. But if authority is not to decline into mere power, it needs constant correction and restraint by the stabilities of the tradition, that pattern of Christian thought and prayer and action which goes deeper than any structure or authority, and of which the saints, not the bishops, are the chief custodians. When all is said and done, Catholicism is about pilgrimage, not about power.

11

Priests For Ever

In one of the prayer books knocking around the house when I was a child there was an ordination card which someone must have given my parents. It had a rather kitsch drawing of a pair of hands elevating the host, and underneath was printed in bold type '*Tu es sacerdos in aeternum, secundum ordinem Melchizedek*': 'You are a priest for ever, after the order of Melchizedek.' I did not at the time realize that this was a misquotation from Hebrews 6, and it was years before I found out who Melchizedek was. All the same, it stuck in my mind, and it came to sum up for me the mystique and timelessness of priesthood. Priesthood was for ever, and to be a priest was to be ordained into a state of life as ancient and unearthly as the Church itself. No priests, no sacraments; and no sacraments, no Church. Christ had invented – or, in view of Melchizedek, maybe reinvented – priests at the Last Supper, ordaining the apostles to say Mass and hear confessions, and that was what priests had gone on doing ever since. The priests who lived in the local parochial house might wear black serge suits, play hurling, and sport bicycle-clips, but in every other respect they were just what the apostles had been, and did just what the apostles did. The clergy, and the work of the clergy, were part of the apostolic timelessness of the Church. They were holy, a race apart, their special status symbolized by and derived from their celibacy.

Nowadays, of course, matters seem not quite so simple. My childhood impressions of the clergy were not foolish, but they represented the absorption and acceptance not of a timeless truth, but of a particular mystique and spirituality of priesthood. What I was brought up to believe in was the Counter-Reformation account of the meaning and nature of ordination. Growing up in Ireland in the 1950s I had no way of knowing that most of those apparently timeless certainties were about to dissolve, and to be called into question. Priesthood, we were about to discover, like all the other institutions of the Church, was a construct, an institution caught, as all human things are caught, in the flux and surge of time.

Celibacy is a case in point. In the last few years a controversy has sputtered on (one can hardly say it has raged) within the Latin Church about the relation of celibacy to priesthood, for Latin Christians are peculiar in having a rule that married men may not be admitted to the priesthood. Orthodox and Eastern Rite Catholics have no such rule, and indeed in the Orthodox tradition parish clergy are expected to marry. Our Latin tradition, however, has located much of the mystique and some of the theological significance of priesthood in the sexual continence and single state of those ordained. This is an emphasis which has roots back to the patristic period – a celibate clergy was an aspiration of some of the early Councils. But for a thousand years it remained largely that, an aspiration. As a practical requirement it dates from the period of the Gregorian reforms of the eleventh century, and in England as in most other places in Europe it was perfectly normal for clergy to marry well into the twelfth and thirteenth centuries. Clerical dynasties, with sons and grandsons succeeding to family clerical posts, were commonplace all over Europe.

But clerical marriage had problems. Nowadays we tend to think about the issue in terms of the sexual symbolism of celibacy. Medieval reforming monks and popes certainly did so too, and they positively shuddered at the thought of a priest whose hands were 'defiled' by sexual activity, touching the sacred elements at the Eucharist. A succession of popes from the time of Leo IX onwards urged the laity to boycott the celebrations of married priests. But there were other more mundane worries. Married clergy needed to provide for their families, and unscrupulous priests and bishops might, and very often did, divert church property to enrich their wives and sons: prams in the presbytery meant hands in the till.

By the end of the Middle Ages that battle had essentially been won: it had been accepted by most people in Western Europe that clergy should be celibate. Not everywhere, of course: from the remoter mountainous regions right down to the eve of the Reformation and beyond we have abundant evidence of widespread acceptance of clerical marriage or concubinage. Peasants made their priests sign contracts guaranteeing that, if they took a wife, it would be a girl from another village, so as not to deplete the stock of marriageable women. But in England at any rate a sterner view prevailed: with some notable exceptions, Cardinal Wolsey chief among them, priests with wives or mistresses found themselves denounced to the bishop and refused employment.

Yet, if clerical celibacy had secured general support, at least in theory, by the time of the Reformation, priests were still a long way from being the holy caste apart of my childhood impressions. Most parish clergy were in fact farmers, like their people grubbing out a living from the land, their boots just as clogged with dung, their minds just as preoccupied with the state of the weather or the price of corn, their values and beliefs very much those of their parishioners. There were no seminaries, and, apart from the monastic life, there were just three basic routes to priesthood. Wealthy men, or those lucky enough to get the backing of a patron, could train in the universities, spending the minimum seven years in the study of theology or canon law (both of them exclusively graduate degrees). Such men, whose training represented an expensive investment, were almost inevitably clerical high-fliers, recruited to staff the great institutions of Church and state. Alternatively, a boy with a good voice might enter a monastic, collegiate or cathedral choir, learn some Latin and theology in the school there, and so progress eventually into the priesthood. For such men, too, a privileged career might lie open. But the overwhelming majority of clergy

acquired the rudiments of clerical knowledge by simple apprenticeship, picking up pidgin Latin and some knowledge of
liturgical practicalities from a local priest (often a relative and, in
the earlier Middle Ages, possibly their father). Such priests
rarely moved far from the areas in which they had been born
and brought up, and they could do little more than celebrate
the essential ceremonies, often stumbling over the Latin of the
rite. (Medieval theologians debated just what degree of gram-
matical confusion was tolerable before a sacrament became
invalid: would a priest who said '*Hocus porpus mecum*' instead of
'*Hoc est corpus meum*' administer the body of the Lord to his
parishioners?) From at least the Fourth Lateran Council (1215),
the local churches were making strenuous efforts to improve
clerical standards, and to ensure that parishioners had priests
who were worthy pastors of souls. The Council's requirement
that the laity should confess their sins to their parish priest at
least once a year led to a sustained campaign to equip clergy to
fulfil the role of confessor, and a flood of books and treatises was
produced to assist the clergy in their pastoral duties. But it was
slow work, on unpromising material: when the English bishops
in 1281 devised a catechetical scheme for the instruction of the
laity, it became universally known by its opening words,
'*Ignorantia sacerdotum*', the ignorance of priests.

Given the low educational and spiritual qualifications of
many of the clergy, the theology of ministry could not be too
high-falutin. Much that we think of as fundamental to the work
of a priest was thought of then as belonging to others. The task
of preaching belonged to the bishops, but after them it was the
special responsibility not of parish priests (though many of them
did in fact preach), but of movements like the friars. The parish
clergy in general were expected only to pass on the most basic
catechetical instruction, and few people thought of the ordinary
clergy as guides of souls or spiritual directors. For such luxuries,
one went to specialists. We get a glimpse of this situation in the
Book of Margery Kempe, the remarkable spiritual autobiography
of an early fifteenth-century townswoman from the major
Norfolk port of Lynn. Margery's book shows her seeking

spiritual guidance from Carmelites, Franciscans, Dominicans, even from the woman hermit Julian of Norwich, but only exceptionally from the clergy in local churches.

Parish clergy baptized, married (though until the Council of Trent the involvement of the clergy in marriage ceremonies was not always thought essential) and buried, they heard annual confessions, they might also teach children their ABC and how to say their prayers. Mostly, however, they were there to provide Masses: more and more of them, as lay appetite for seeing the Host (most people took Communion only once a year, at Easter) grew. Most clergy were part of an impoverished clerical proletariat, dressing much like laymen, eking out a moonlight existence by saying Mass for money. In many parts of Europe by the end of the Middle Ages, not least in much of Germany, there were far too many priests, scraping around for a living, some of them given to pestering women or boys for sexual favours, resented by the laity at large for their legal and tax privileges, their rootless lifestyle, and their non-involvement in civic responsibility. In England, by contrast, the evidence suggests that a reasonable balance had been achieved. Here, by and large, the clergy were seen as providing services which the people valued – the Mass and the sacraments, above all, but also teaching in local schools, acting as scribes in communities where most people could neither read nor write, and organizing musical and dramatic life, part of the accepted order of things.

Naturally, the advent of Protestantism changed all that, by challenging the multiplication of Masses which had led to the great expansion in clerical numbers. And, even in Catholic countries, the sixteenth century brought reform. The Council of Trent sought to renew the Church at diocesan and parish level, and to achieve that renewal the Fathers of the Council understood that they would need a new and better type of priest. The Tridentine priest was to be one who lived among his people and for his people, but who was not of his people, a man in fact a cut above them educationally, spiritually, morally. This was a spiritual vision, not a class-based one, for Trent laid it down that candidates for the priesthood should ideally come from among the poor. But ordinands were to be taken at an early age – 12 was normal – and whisked away from their village to a special 'seed-bed' or hothouse for training priests, the new invention of the diocesan seminary. There they would wear a cassock, shave their heads, live a disciplined, ordered routine apart from the people, and acquire a clericalized spiritual and educational culture. They would be properly trained in theology and morals, and indoctrinated in a clerical lifestyle, so that when they returned to their parishes they would be equipped both to teach and to inspire by example, and they would be less easily absorbed back into local culture and local values.

Trent's vision (which owes much to the ideas developed for use in England by Mary Tudor's Archbishop of Canterbury, Cardinal Pole) took centuries to achieve – Pope Benedict XIV was still trying to force southern Italian dioceses to establish seminaries for the first time in the 1740s. But as more and more seminaries came into existence in the late sixteenth and seventeenth centuries, a new type of priest emerged – more pious, more professional, better educated, above all much more clerical. A key figure here was St Charles Borromeo, Archbishop of Milan in the late sixteenth century, who deliberately set himself to discipline his clergy into model parish priests, and who published a stream of synodal acts and spiritual treatises designed to provide the clergy of Europe with models of behaviour, and with pastoral resources.

In seventeenth-century France activists like St Vincent de Paul brought about a transformation of clerical standards and attitudes, and in the process evolved a new clerical spirituality. As the parish clergy came to be seen as primarily responsible for the shaping of the religious life of the people, the dignity of the secular priesthood came more and more to be asserted. Monks and friars were all very well, but their state of life had not been instituted by Christ: the priesthood had. So it was the parish clergy, not the 'specialist' monks, friars or Jesuits, who should be the main directors of souls. In the Middle Ages the annual obligation to confess to one's parish priest was often a routinized matter of ensuring that everyone performed a minimal duty. Anyone with inclination and leisure enough to aspire to something more would be likely to seek it in a monastery or friary. Now, however, the regular and more frequent contact between penitent and parish priest acting as confessor and adviser came to be seen as potentially the single most important pastoral weapon in a priest's armoury. More and more the simple country priest became the focus of theologizing, and the dignity of priesthood was more and more exalted. The priest, it was said, was as holy and privileged as the Virgin herself, for like her the priest brought Christ into the world – as one English Counter-Reformation writer, Thomas White, declared:

> Consider, of how much dignity it is, and honour, to have received the administering of God himself, to bear him in your hands, to have him in your power, to give him to whom you will . . . see how the priest hath received that which is not granted to the Angels, nor was ever lawful to any but only to his blessed Mother.

The humble massing-priest of the Middle Ages, a sort of spiritual plumber called in only to do a job and paid off at the servant's entrance, had acquired a mystique formerly limited to the religious. In the process, the priesthood was monasticized – clerical training, clerical dress, clerical culture, clerical spirituality were all designed to mark off the priest's vocation and state of life as unique, mysterious, awesome in its responsibility and privilege. Friendships between priests and their parishioners were discouraged (only partly in the interests of maintaining celibacy). The priest was indeed like Melchizedek, without parentage, without roots, a man apart from other men (and especially women!).

It was a noble ideal, and carried with it the notion of the priest as lonely spiritual warrior or explorer, spending long days and nights on his knees, suffering for his people, enduring loneliness and spiritual pain for their sakes. A sense of what this

might mean at its most intense, the priest as a man with Christ
in the Garden of Gethsemane, can be drawn from reading
George Bernanos' classic novel *The Diary of a Country Priest*. But
it was a vision of priesthood which depended for its coherence
on a sense of uniqueness and separation in priestly vocation, not
easily compatible with the more corporate ecclesiology put
forward by theologians like Karl Adam, Henri de Lubac and
Yves Congar before the Council, and canonized in the
Conciliar constitution on the Church, *Lumen gentium*. It was
also dependent on a particular sociology, in which priests were
better educated or at any rate differently educated from their
people, and in which the confessional was understood as a
regular and frequent place of direction and guidance: the priest
as spiritual expert and spiritual master. And it was dependent on
sociology in other ways, too. If it was to work, the Counter-
Reformation ideal of priesthood needed its markers of
separation: the tonsure, the dog-collar and cassock, the locked
presbytery, the emotional distance between priest and people,
the use of clerical titles, celibacy. These were not optional
extras, they were part of the fabric of that particular Counter-
Reformation understanding of priesthood.

By contrast, we increasingly demand of our clergy that they
should be animators, not masters, that they should be approach-
able, friendly, involved, on first-name terms. There is often
among lay people a cruel naïveté about the demands that these
new expectations place on clergy. We need to understand the
scale of Trent's achievement, in its refashioning and elevation of
priesthood, but we need also to grasp the price and the methods
which that achievement demanded. We need also to understand
that the Tridentine vision is slowly but surely collapsing under
the joint pressures of theological and social change. Without
Tridentine structures and attitudes, we cannot have Tridentine
priesthood: we cannot have our cake and eat it.

The Middle Ages had a vision of priesthood which was
modest and limited. The priest was to be to the Church what
the local blacksmith or carpenter was to the secular community,
a conscientious workman providing essential services. He must

provide with decency the sacraments and sacramentals, he must instil the bare essentials of Christian doctrine and morals into his people, dispense charity to the poor, make peace when neighbours quarrelled, avoid open scandal in his private life. He was not expected to be a preacher, or a guru, nor indeed, in any very serious sense, a spiritual expert of any sort.

Trent and the Counter-Reformation had a different, more exalted vision. The priest was to be a man apart for the people, but, it followed, also a man apart *from* the people: his life must be conformed to the miracle he performed each day at the altar. He was to be a man of prayer, an example of personal sanctity. He was to be expert in theology and ethics, a spiritual guide to others, and the voice of a teaching *magisterium* which was ever more detailed and comprehensive in its concerns. When in doubt, you should ask the priest. He was, in fact, to be what the Middle Ages had expected in a monk, though he was expected to live without the support of community.

Our present system of clerical training was designed to provide that sort of priest: it is the product of the Tridentine moment, a moment that lasted from 1560 to 1960, and those of us whose Catholicism was formed by it owe it a profound debt of gratitude. But the Tridentine moment is passing, perhaps has already passed. The sort of expertise the Tridentine priest was expected to have is now within the reach of us all, and in the West we do not need or at any rate no longer want the sort of clerical guru which Trent set itself to produce. As society changes, as the Church calls on all the laity to claim and exercise their priesthood, and as we discover that the charisms which help form the life of the Church can be given to all and not just to the clergy, we are confronted with an urgent need to reimagine the ordained priesthood, as the Counter-Reformation reimagined and reinvented it. It is a task which makes some of the current debate over the ordination of women seem relatively minor, and somewhat premature.

12

The Art of Dying

Catholics used to think a lot about death. One of the earliest prayers I learned was a prayer for the grace of a happy death – it carried, I remember, an indulgence of 300 days every time you said it, and we said it every day:

> Jesus, Mary and Joseph, I give you my heart and my soul:
> Jesus, Mary and Joseph, assist me in my last agony:
> Jesus, Mary and Joseph, may I breathe forth my soul in
>   peace with you.
> Amen.

St Joseph was the patron saint of the dying because Mary and the child Jesus had been at his death-bed (a fact deduced from Joseph's absence from the Gospels after the infancy narratives). Or rather, he was the patron not so much of the dying, but of a 'good' or a 'happy' death, for that was the point of the prayer. Everyone would die, but what mattered was a 'good' death.

Not many people are likely to make much sense of the notion of a 'good' or a 'happy' death. I remember being profoundly shocked when a clerical (though non-Catholic) friend told me he'd like to die eating chips on a bus on the way back from a football match, and I suspect most people nowadays, Catholic or not, would opt for some such notion of a 'good' death. For us, life is about living, and death is just the end of living, something which hardly bears thinking about, and only the morbid dwell on.

But back then, in Ireland in the 1950s, that was not what we meant at all. In the town where I was born, death was a community event, and funerals regularly halted the traffic on the main Dublin–Belfast road. And when anyone died in our area all the children were rounded up and taken to see the corpse in its open coffin. There were routines of death: women who did the laying out, prayers to be said when you came to view the corpse, holy water to be sprinkled. The Victorian crucifix I keep on my study table was part of my grandmother's 'laying-out set', kept on a high shelf along with its linen runner, candlesticks and holy-water bowl, and brought out only for death-beds and sick visits. Death was expected, familiar, contained and controlled by rituals and routines which named even if they could not tame it.

In that culture, death was a public event, and a 'good' death meant a death properly prepared for, fortified with the rites of holy church, having made peace with God and neighbour. More than that, the moment of death was not the sputtering out of life, it was not the last thing that happened to us: it was itself the climax of the Christian life, the performance for which everything else had been the rehearsal. This was not mere folk custom, it was a reflection of a considered theology. The Jesuit theologian Ladislaus Boros wrote a moving book on the theology of dying, called *The Moment of Truth*, and the title captures what it was we were encouraged to think about the act of dying. This was the moment which would show what we were, and which would determine our eternal destiny.

> As the tree falls, so shall it lie;
> As a man lives, so shall he die:
> As a man dies, so shall he be,
> Through all the aeons of eternity.

If modern Catholics find all this a bit difficult, it is in part because we inhabit a radically different dramatic conception of life and death. In our culture, death is a non-event, taking place, preferably, off-stage and out of sight in a hospital ward, ideally when we are asleep or unconscious, emphatically not public. Even 40 years ago, when the sociologist Geoffrey Gorer published his survey *Death, Grief and Mourning*, he uncovered the shocking fact that most parents whose children died in British hospitals were not at their child's bedside at the moment of death. Death is a switching-off, a nothing. Our culture now has few rituals for dealing with death, as anyone who has been to a crematorium funeral will know. But we have even fewer rituals for dying, apart from those of the secular desolation of the hospital ward. When the poet John Betjeman, who was haunted by the fear of death, wrote about his own death-bed in one of his most terrifying poems, he evoked the 'moment of truth' in a chilling phrase which exactly catches our situation:

> say, in what cottage hospital,
> *when they range the screens around.*

Death is something to be screened, and in the process the moment of death has been stripped of its ceremony, and its comforts. My son spent some time a few years ago as an auxiliary geriatric nurse in a great hospital: one of the things he discovered was that clergy visits to the dying were not encouraged, because, allegedly, they frightened the other patients.

It was otherwise in the culture of Tridentine and pre-Tridentine catholicism. Death was something which we would all not only have to suffer, it was something we would all have to *do*. We were required to die our deaths, and that dying was itself an act and a moment charged both with danger and with promise. The moment of death was not a blind alley, but a threshold between worlds, over which the Christian was launched with an army of supporters:

> Go forth upon thy journey Christian soul,
> Go from this world,
> Go in the name of God, the omnipotent father who
>   created thee
> In the name of angels and archangels, thrones and
>   dominations, princedoms and powers.

Medieval Christians believed that the devil's final and most desperate temptations were reserved for the last days and hours of the dying Christian, and the death-bed was the scene of a cosmic struggle for the soul, the stages of which could be and were carefully charted.

In the fifteenth century a world best-selling treatise emerged, called *The Art of Dying*, an extraordinary phrase which encapsulated a whole theology of death seen not as something merely suffered, but something which we ourselves *did*. Boiled down into 11 pictures, it portrayed the five great temptations which the devil would launch at the dying Christian, together with their antidotes – despair versus hope, impatience versus resignation, presumption or pride versus humble trust in Christ and the saints, and so on. The book reached every corner of Europe, and affected the routines of the death-bed and the pastoral practice of the Church.

Dying Christians had a clear set of duties – to sort out their worldly debts and duties, to make up any quarrels, to profess the orthodox Catholic faith, to receive the last sacraments, to die in the public manifestation of trust in God. In all this the help – and the presence – of family, friends and neighbours was hoped for and expected. Death beds were public, not private occasions. Sudden and unprepared death, death which denied the Christian proper opportunity for all these duties, became the most dreaded fate. People practised indulgenced devotions to which miraculous promises of a guaranteed 'good' death were attached – the 'Nine First Fridays' was one modern example of such devotions, which have a pedigree back into the Middle Ages. Miracle stories spread of long-dead corpses being revived by the special intercession of the Virgin Mary, simply so that they could die properly, and so gain heaven. For Mary was the supreme saint of the death-bed, hence the familiar petition in the second part of the 'Hail Mary', added at the end of the Middle Ages, 'Pray for us sinners now and *at the hour of our death*'.

This may all seem a bit unreal. Death is not always, probably not often, a timely and dignified affair, allowing the patriarch to take his leave of the gathered family. Christians then as now knew perfectly well that many of us don't have the luck to be in charge of our own dying. Even before the twenty-first century people suffered heart attacks, had seizures on the lavatory, fell off scaffolding, were trampled by runaway horses, or at the crucial moment were simply asleep, comatose, or distracted by pain, unable to concentrate their mind on the great business of dying. And so it was felt that somehow life should be shaped by dying, that the whole of life should be a practice for the final moment. We must die daily, so that we are always ready whenever the actual moment of death arrived. So, somewhat spectacularly, certain kinds of monks and nuns slept in their coffins, saintly bishops kept skulls on their desks, and the rest of us prayed to Jesus, Mary and Joseph for the grace of a happy death. Bishop Challenor's *Penny Catechism* instructed (and instructs) every lay person to compose themselves as if for death last thing each night when they lie down in bed, a frame of mind which must have been a serious damper of enthusiasm for any married couples who took it seriously. Many of us, in short, were brought up in a form of Christianity where mortification – literally, deadening – was at a premium.

Clearly, a lot of this has to do with people living in a rawer, more vulnerable society, where death was closer and more threatening than it is for most of us. The death rate is, of course, the same in every society – 100 per cent. But until modern times – as still in the developing world – people might die younger than most of us can expect to, there were fewer barriers against disease or natural disaster, and so fewer people made it to the biblical three-score and ten. That does not, however, really account for the profoundly different response to the fact of death between Christian culture then and now. For Christians now, like everybody else, live as if each one of us were immortal. Our dominant forms of spirituality often emphasize the way in which the gospel enhances *life*. Just consider the ways in which a slogan like 'holiness equals wholeness' (surely the most detestable of modern heresies, in wild contradiction of the fact that so many holy people have been blatantly neurotic or maladjusted) can be used to focus the pursuit of holiness on a this-worldly understanding of the good life.

There has been some sort of conceptual or imaginative shift in modern Christianity, which has made death and dying very hard for us to handle, and makes us resistant to placing dying near the centre of our spiritual perceptions. To some extent this is a good thing. For centuries Christians effectively replaced the doctrine of the resurrection of the body with the doctrine of 'the after-life'. Human existence was seen as unproblematically continuous before and after death: anyone over 40 will remember pious stories of death-beds where the dying person sits up and holds out their arms to greet a long-dead loved one, or the Blessed Virgin, or their guardian angel, come to escort them to the other world as they 'cross over' to the other side. What mattered was the soul, and the soul slipped relatively easily out of the body at death and got on with its existence. The 'moment of truth' was in fact the moment when the soul woke up to its true nature. This sort of imagery may have a use, but we need to be aware how 'untraditional' it is, and how profoundly unbiblical. It runs the danger of emptying death of its total destructiveness, what Newman called 'the masterful negation and collapse of all that makes me man'. Even more, it runs the risk of robbing the resurrection of Christ of its stupendous re-creating power.

To the extent that it prevents us taking 'survival' for granted, then, our failure of nerve about death, the passing away within even Christian culture of a strongly imagined sense of the after-life, may be a gain. But not if it leaves us unable to own our deaths, to claim them as part of what we are, as something we can and must do.

Death happens to us, whether we like it or not, whether we acknowledge it or not: one day we will be taken where we do not want to go. To that extent we certainly don't do it, it does for us. But the Christian tradition's insistence that we must nevertheless own our deaths, that we must *do* our dying, as an act of faith hope and love, is not an attempt to hang on to control. Christ 'lays down his life', his death is something 'accomplished', and so must ours be. This has nothing in common with euthanasia or suicide, which are attempts not merely to own our deaths, but to be lords over death. Instead it is an acceptance of mortality as part of what we are, a willing and willed surrender of our lives to the God who gives life, an act of trust that all that we are and all we do, even the last thing, even the moment in which we are undone, has meaning and shape in the heart of God, and is part of his work in us.

My family recently suffered the loss of two beloved parents, both people of exceptional goodness and faith, yet for both of whom the process of dying – the steady erosion of mobility, ability to concentrate and to enjoy, the dwindling not only of zest but even of the will to live, the constant presence of pain – was a source of great suffering. For both of them the acceptance of that process, submitting to be bound and taken where they did not want to go, was a hard test of their discipleship.

It was the wisdom of the tradition of the 'good death' that it grasped that our faith cannot speak truly about life unless it also speaks about death. If faith itself is a loving belief and trust in the truth of God and his promises, then the surrender involved in coming to terms with our own dying is an integral part of it. And if our style of Christianity has little to say about that surrender, there is something badly amiss.

To allow our deaths to inhere in and inform the patterns of our lives has no necessary connotations of morbidity, though in cultural terms morbidity has been a danger to which Christians have often succumbed – one thinks of the absurd early Wesleyan hymn:

> O lovely appearance of death,
> No sight upon earth is so fair,
> Not all the gay pageants that breathe
> Can with a dead body compare.

We should not be in love with death, but in some sense we do need to be able to embrace it. In one of his most powerful novels, *Pincher Martin*, William Golding portrays the process of damnation precisely as the inability of the novel's central (indeed only) character to accept the reality of his own death. Pincher Martin is a shipwrecked sailor, apparently stranded on a rock in mid-ocean. As the novel progresses we realize that Martin's frantic struggle for life is the culmination and epitome of a lifelong ruthlessness which has refused to make space for anything or anyone except his own ego. Death, the 'black-lightening' which he tries to hold at bay, is a sacrament of surrender, an opportunity for true humanity, but one which he refuses. Only in the last lines of the novel do we learn that Martin has been dead all along, the island with its pools and promontories merely the contours of his teeth, the terrible struggle for survival is no more than the final shrinking into itself of a consciousness unable to open to the reality of others.

At the heart of our faith there hangs a man portrayed, in the dominant Western artistic tradition, in the very act of dying. There has been only one truly good death, one death 'freely accepted', and it happened on Calvary. But it has been a consistent part of Christian teaching that discipleship in some sense involves the imitation of that death, and that free acceptance. Imitation involves art, the conscious following of a pattern, and that needs to be practised and worked at. We need not, should not, imitate the cultural forms in which the art of dying has been expressed in the past, any more than we need imitate the crepe bands and black ostrich-feathers of Victorian funerals. But we should not imagine that the imitation of this aspect of the Christian mystery comes without effort, or the conscious effort of art. We must discover for ourselves, and together, what it might mean for our times to imitate the pattern of Christ's dying within the life of the Church.

And the old forms have life in them yet. Any Christian culture which distances us from a sense of our own mortality cuts us off from participation in Christ's dying. It cuts us off also from solidarity with those for whom death is an unavoidable present reality, who hang with him on his cross – the truly poor, the famine-stricken, the powerless. Medieval and Baroque

Catholicism sometimes imagined death, it is true, primarily in individualistic terms, as the end of *my* conscious bodily life. Meditations on the last things were often designed to portray the very processes of dissolution, the terrors, discomforts and pains of dying. The object was to shock the individual into a reform of life, a more intense piety, to save her soul. Devotional texts on dying often portrayed it, therefore, as a supremely lonely experience. But the Christian imagination of death need not be socially alienating or individualistic in this way. The principal means by which the tradition urged Christians to make real a sense of their own death – fasting, self-denial – are in fact well suited to a more vivid realization of our mortality, and hence of our solidarity with the bulk of the world's dying, for whom fasting is not a devotional luxury but a fact of life – and death.

13

An Apology for Grief,
Fear and Anger

We are accustomed to thinking of the liturgical reforms which
have flowed from the Second Vatican Council as essentially to
do with translation and, in many cases, simplification. The
doctrine stays the same, but is made more accessible. In fact,
however, anyone who sits down with the old Roman Missal
and compares it with its modern counterpart, text by text, will
soon realize that in countless cases there has been a real and in
some cases startling shift, which is all too often a doctrinal loss.
The prayers of the new rite in English are usually vaguer but
more optimistic than the 'originals' they 'translate', and the
theological tension which the best of the old Roman prayers
possessed has fairly consistently been smoothed and simplified
away. If one sought to characterize the spirit of the old rite, one
would probably point to its austerity, a sombre sense underlying
many of its prayers of the ambivalence of worldly happiness, and
a sense of human frailty and sinfulness, offset by an emphasis on
God's grace. Little of this could be said of the spirit of the
present Roman rite.

Anyone who doubts the contrast should try comparing the
old Latin collect for the third Sunday after Pentecost, *Protector
in Te Sperantium*, with the modern version, we find on new
missals, for the seventeenth Sunday of Year B, 'God our Father
and Protector'. Here is the old prayer:

*Protector in te sperantium Deus: sine quo nihil est validum, nihil
sanctum: multiplica super nos misericordiam tuam, ut te rectore te*

duce, sic transeamus per bona temporalia, ut non amittamus aeterna. Per Dominium Nostrum I.C.

Thomas Cranmer in the Book of Common Prayer translated this *almost* perfectly:

> God the protector of all that trust in thee, without whom nothing is strong, nothing is holy; increase and multiply upon us thy mercy; that thou being our ruler and guide, we may so pass through things temporal, that we finally lose not the things eternal. Grant this, heavenly father for Jesus Christ sake.

The original prayer is carefully balanced between affirmation and renunciation. It is a prayer which affirms the goodness of God's world, and at the same time points to its dangers: the pivot of the prayer is the phrase *sic transeamus per bona temporalia*. The things of this world are good, but have to be passed through. We are to be pilgrims, because if we settle for the good things of this world, we will lose ourselves, and God, in them. Cranmer's version falls down perhaps in not sufficiently bringing out the meaning of the phrase *bona temporalia*: his version is not affirmative enough of this world, and so the urgency of the *transeamus*, the need to keep moving, is lost. To us who live in a grossly materialist culture, which rates people's value by their earning and spending power, and assesses human happiness by the possession of good things, it is difficult to imagine a more salutary and necessary emphasis. Now consider the current version.

> God our Father and Protector, without you nothing is holy, nothing has value. Guide us to everlasting life by helping us to use wisely the blessings you have given to the world.

The whole tension of the original prayer, its balance between the goodness of the world on the one hand, and its ability to conceal from us the creator, to trap us, on the other, is here abandoned. The notion of *danger*, and the sense of *journeying* are gone. All that is left is a rather banal prayer for the sensible use of a good creation. No message here for post-Thatcher Britain.

It is easy to see why this has come about. To those of us brought up in the Catholicism of the 1950s or earlier, it did often seem that sin, misery and suffering had more than their share of our attention as Catholics, and the liturgy often seemed stuck in the penitential groove. The radical Catholic magazine *Slant*, of blessed memory, used to run a column of ghastly extracts from Catholic publications which it called 'The Real Thing'. I remember one of these, from a parish magazine somewhere in America, was a series of contrasts between 'us' and 'them', 'them' being Protestants. One of these ran, 'Catholic crucified Christ, YES! Protestant risen Christ, NO! ' A travesty, of course, but one with something in it.

It was therefore almost inevitable that when the liturgy came to be re-shaped in the wake of the Council, an attempt would be made to correct this excessive emphasis on the negative. By and large the resulting gain outweighs the loss. The new liturgy offers a much more balanced exposure to the full range of scripture, and Sunday worship has recovered its proper Easter character. But the price for this undoubted gain has sometimes been very high, and nowhere more than in the liturgy of the dead.

Funerals and the other rites of the dead before the present reforms were certainly sombre affairs – the priest's vestments and the altar-hangings were purple or black, the liturgy drew on passages of scripture which emphasized the fear of judgement, the terror of death itself, and need for mercy. For most people, I suppose, the text that focused all this was the *Dies Irae*, that terrifying hymn originally written for use in Advent but which had somehow found its way into the funeral Mass, so that the tremendous imagery of the end of the world, that 'Day of wrath and Doom impending', was brought to bear on every individual death.

> What terror on each breast shall lie
> When downward from the bending sky
> The judge shall come our souls to try.

It could be argued, indeed it was repeatedly argued, that all this was a very bad thing: it encouraged people to be afraid of their redeemer, to concentrate on their own sinfulness rather than on the grace of God, and it made death harder to come to terms with. And so the new liturgy of the dead has swept most of this away. The concern of the new rite is to console the living by an insistence on the trusting confidence of the Church in a God who has shown himself in Christ to be a God of Love. The replacement of black vestments by others in colours chosen 'to express Christian hope', though with the proviso that they must not be offensive 'to human grief or sorrow', is one of the ways in which the rite seeks to emphasize that a Christian death is not to be the source of fear, but an occasion of hope. The scripture readings prescribed for use at funeral Masses and the other offices of the dead consistently emphasize trust, hope, the mercy of God, the joy of the resurrection. There are here certainly real and valuable manifestations of a more evangelical spirit.

But, alas, that is not all they are. They also represent a sanitizing and impoverishment of the liturgy of the dead, an emptying out of the complexity and depth it needs to possess. My own conviction is that, as in the case of the collect we examined earlier, the whole process represents a timid and unimaginative, and therefore theologically defective, flattening of the rites of the dead into two dimensions. We are in danger of depriving the liturgy of the dead of true universality by making it capable of expressing only a small range of theologically contrived and approved responses to death.

Consider the implications of removing from the funeral rite the *Dies Irae*. In its old position, the *Dies Irae* served two functions. It expressed real, gut-churning human fear in the face of death and the eternal, and it also linked the fate of the individual, in a stark and inescapable way, with the universal reality of judgement, a judgement which embraced in the hymn not only the material universe, but the whole of human society. The hymn spoke, as our new rite never does, with intense and sobering seriousness about the possibility of eternal loss. It therefore took seriously, as again the new rites do not, the reality of human sin, not least the sins of society against its victims, evoked in the imagery of the parable about the victim poor, from Matthew 25:

> *Inter oves locum praesta*
> *Et ab hoedis me sequestra*
> *Statuens in parte dextra.*

> With thy sheep a place provide me,
> From the goats afar divide me,
> To thy right hand do thou guide me.

It is characteristic of our individualistic culture that it was the likely psychological effect of this hymn which most often led liturgists to cast a disapproving eye on it, and which helped determine its abandonment. Its universal scope, its admittedly formidable but deeply scriptural association of this death, and the moral worth of this life, with the universal, with justice and human destiny on the grandest scale, have been sacrificed too lightly. I am not arguing for the restoration of this Latin hymn, or any of its rather poor English versions, to funeral Masses. But the things which the *Dies Irae* represented and kept before us at the solemn and terrible moment of the loss of loved ones, need to be present in Christian mourning.

Or consider, again, the disappearance of the element of anger, complaint and protest from the new rites of the dead.

The old breviary office for the dead, known from the opening word of its first psalm *Dirige domine* as the *Dirge*, was one of the most magnificently constructed services in the whole of the liturgy. It was organized around a series of psalms which alternated between expressions of fear, anger and dismay in the face of death, and of comfort, reassurance and trust. These psalms were arranged in three groups, or 'nocturns', and accompanied three sets of three readings, nine in all, from the book of Job. The passages from Job, put in the context of funeral liturgy, were astonishing. They explored the whole gamut of human feeling in the face of suffering and death: fear, anger, self-justification, reproach, longing for relief, trust, affirmation. One of the most remarkable emphases in the readings is that of bitterness and complaint against God:

My soul is weary of life, I will speak in the bitterness of
    my soul
I will say to God, do not condemn me, let me know
    why you contend against me
Does it seem good to you to oppress me, to despise the
    work of your hands?
Your hands have made me, and fashioned me about, and
    yet now you destroy me
Are your years as the years of men, that you should seek
    my iniquity, and search out my sin?

None of this has survived in the new liturgy. The complaints of Job were, evidently, too challenging for inclusion, seen as negative, disrespectful or otherwise unsuitable. Yet one of the principal functions of liturgy is to allow us to pray all our thoughts and feelings, to acknowledge before God what we really are, not to suppress and sanitize our innermost selves and only bring to him what is acceptable and theologically 'correct'. That bitter note of protest is surely one of the most basic of human responses to death, and one of the most legitimate; it is one which we can hear echoed in the cry from the cross, 'Why have you forsaken me?'

Like the removal of the *Dies Irae*, the silencing of the voice of protest against God in the face of our own death or those of our loved ones makes the note of consolation and hope in the new rite more consistent, but in the process and as the price renders the liturgical response of the Christian to death two-dimensional. Our trust and hope in God must take the measure of our fear and doubt. By speaking only of the positive feelings we *should* have in the face of death, the new liturgy gives no scope for us to confront and acknowledge in prayer, and so to find healing for all those negative feelings which so often surface in the face of bereavement. Anger with ourselves, with God, with the loved one who has left us; guilt, before God and about the unfinished business which so often remains between us and the dead one, however much loved; and raw grief, which will not be, and should not be, easily and quickly fobbed off with reassurance and 'correct' theology. We need to come to the knowledge that 'my redeemer liveth', but we need also to be allowed to rage against the dying of the light. The old liturgy made space for both: the new does not. Moreover, the new liturgy of death seems ill-fitted for the use of those for whom death is not the relatively tidy affair we imagine the 'normal' death to be, in the quiet seclusion of a hospital bed, at the end of a long and reasonably stable life. Sudden death, violent death, unjust death, cruel death: these find little voice or acknowledgement. And yet for the majority of our brothers and sisters, these are the most familiar shapes of death. The uniform composure, resignation and trust of the new liturgy are the expression of a particular, and I would say profoundly provincial and unrepresentative cultural experience of death.

If this be so, can a liturgy which claims to be Catholic afford to carry so large a hidden agenda? Must the most traumatic dimension of our common tragedy as human beings remain silent and permanently submerged, flickering at the edge of our field of vision, but given only a sanitized and softened expression in our ritual encounter with the mystery of death? The welcome emphasis of the new liturgy on hope, trust and confidence has been secured at the cost of suppressing terror, the sense of waste, tragedy, the sheer bloody meaninglessness of mortality. The banishment of mourning vestments, of the *Dies Irae*, of the open expression in the liturgy of fear, loss and a sense of punishment, prevent our funeral rites from acting as a truly prayerful expression of our full experience of death, what Newman called 'The masterful negation and collapse of all that makes me man.'

The motives behind this clean-up operation are presumably similar to those at work in the bowdlerization of the Psalms in the Divine Office in general. Whatever they are, they have resulted in the presentation as universal of religious rites, conceived in terms dictated by societies like our own in which death is believed or pretended to happen peacefully (or at least out of view) and mostly to the sick or elderly. The absence of fear, anguish and anger from the ritual ensures that it cannot serve to discharge those emotions in the mourner, nor, more momentously, serve as an act of solidarity with the mourning of those for whom death is a more devouring and uncontrollable visitation – the result of oppression or mass famine, of life lived, as much human life is lived, at the limits.

I am not pleading for any straightforward revival of the 'Tridentine' liturgy of death. For most people the forms of that liturgy have probably become culturally unusable, and mere antiquarianism could not restore to the funeral rites the actual complexity and range that I have been arguing need to be present there. Nor am I arguing that funerals should become crude therapy sessions, with raw emotions manipulated and stirred by shock tactics, half-baked psychology designed to make people purge themselves with a good cry. The value of the older service was precisely that it handled these potentially devastating feelings within the formal control of ritual. But we urgently need to discover ways of making our burial rites less bland, less didactic, less easily reassuring. Without sacrificing the emphasis on Christian hope and resurrection which the new rite has brought out so clearly, we need to make room for the expression of darker and less easily acknowledged feelings and fears: it may be that the mere restoration of some of the suppressed readings from Job, and some of the craggier Psalms from the old rite, might do much to fulfil the lack. But something needs to be done, if our Christian response to death is not to appear, and to be, superficial and cheaply optimistic, seeking to comfort and reassure without entering into the darkness in which most of us confront the reality of death.

14

Praying for the Dead

I grew up in the 1950s in a small town on the east coast of Ireland. Neither my family nor the wider community struck me, then or since, as specially pious, but religion was everywhere, and it was a religion in which the dead were more or less continuously present. Collection boxes stood at the back of every church for 'the Holy Souls'. The dead were remembered as part of every public prayer, even grace before meals, which always ended with petitions for eternal rest and light perpetual on the souls of the faithful departed. Our prayer books were stuffed with memorial cards, pious bookmarks whose stilted inscriptions and blurred photographs reminded us of the obligation to pray for departed friends and relatives. Every year at Easter we walked in a straggling procession the mile or more to the town cemetery for the annual blessing of the graves: the week before was a period of intensive clearing and tidying of family plots, in which it would be hard to say whether grief, devotion or the determination not to let the family down in front of the neighbours had the upper hand. November 2nd, All Souls Day, was not a holiday of obligation, but everyone with any pretensions to religion went to Mass, the liturgy notable for the sombre black vestments in which the celebrant was swathed, and the De La Salle brothers who ran our local school explained that we could gain an indulgence which would release a soul from purgatory during every visit to a church that day in the course of which we recited five 'Our Fathers' and five 'Hail Marys' for the pope's intentions. There was no limit on how many times this indulgence could be gained, so the pious or the elderly with a lot of dead friends and relatives could be seen going in and out of church all day long, chalking up the indulgences, the wing-beats of the ransomed beating joyously about their ears.

Behind all this was a very clear geography of the afterlife, charting every detail of the fate of the departed. That geography had taken a thousand years to evolve. There is little or no explicit mention of prayer for the dead in the New Testament, but invocations for the peace of the departed occur among the earliest Christian grave inscriptions, and the dead are commemorated in ancient liturgical texts like the Canon of the Mass. A few theologians, like St Augustine and St Gregory the Great, speculated about the existence of a state of painful purgation by fire through which the imperfectly or belatedly penitent must pass before they were granted the beatific vision, but a full-blown theology of purgatory did not emerge until the beginning of the second millennium. Here, as so often in Christian history, theory lagged well behind practice. The Western liturgy of mourning for and commemoration of the dead reached its decisive form not in the parishes or dioceses of the Church at large, but in the monasteries of the Middle Ages. There, in close-knit communities in which the memories of dead brethren were lovingly cherished, and in which there were large numbers of religious and priests with time to pray, intercession for the dead came to be seen as one of the chief obligations — and benefits — of monastic life. Soon the lay patrons, benefactors and clients of the monasteries sought a share in this benefit, paying to have their names included on the lists of those prayed for in the monasteries, even acquiring graves in monastic precincts. The liturgy of the wider Church began to absorb and imitate the services of intercession for the dead evolved in the monasteries, and the monastic office for the dead became an essential component even of lay prayer books.

Alongside this liturgical and devotional development went a legal and theological rationale. How did prayer benefit the dead? Theologians elaborated the theory of a middle state

between heaven and hell, in which all those who had died in a
state of grace but imperfectly purged of the aftermath of sin
would be cleansed and prepared for heaven. Western theology
had long since adopted an essentially forensic or legal account of
sin and forgiveness. Sin repented of would not exclude from
heaven, but it left behind an aftermath, a burden of damages or
of 'satisfaction' to be worked off in acts of penance – self-denial
and self-punishment, charity to the poor, prayer. The theological kernel of this development was the annual Christian
experience of Lent, in which the whole community fasted and
prayed and gave to the poor in reparation for its sins, and in
search of renewal. But 'satisfaction' was conceived primarily in
punitive rather than in therapeutic terms, and early medieval
penitentials worked out fixed tariffs to calculate the amount of
penance required – mandatory sentences for sins of varying
degrees of seriousness.

But what of those who died with such penance incomplete?
Purgatory was the answer to that question, imagined as a period
of time granted or imposed after death in which the unfinished
business of satisfactory penance could be completed. The
prayers of those still on earth, and works of penance or of
charity carried out on behalf of or in solidarity with the dead,
could shorten this period of post-mortem penance, and this, it
was thought, explained the Church's immemorial custom of
praying for the dead. The perception was reflected in devotion.
Where the prayers for the dead in the early Church were mostly
petitions for rest, light and peace, death imagined as a sailing
into rest in which the dead were accompanied by the loving
memories of the living, the memorial prayers of the Middle
Ages were mostly cast as prayers for release from suffering, an
emphasis not unknown in antiquity but coming into its own
now in response to the elaborated speculations of the theologians.

But not only of the theologians. The Christian imagination
had been at work on the nature of this 'purgatory'. The picture-
language of the Bible on the afterlife suggested essentially
two scenarios, a paradise garden of bliss for those in heaven, a

cellar-full of torments for those in hell. Since purgatory was the place where sin was punished and removed, it was felt it must resemble hell more than heaven. And 'place' was the operative words: most of those who reflected on the subject thought it must be a real place, a prison which was part of the geography of hell, only not quite so deep or dark, and with exits available when the sentence was complete. Thus purgatory at its crudest (and it was an idea which was often crudely conceived) was imagined as an out-patients' department of hell, staffed by demons, to whose power every Christian soul would be for a time delivered, to undergo savage but finite torments as a just punishment for unexpiated sins. St Brigid of Sweden, a canonized visionary who left what purported to be eyewitness accounts of the ferocious sufferings of purgatory, reported that there were even people there who had been allowed by God to think themselves in hell, their mistaken despair of damnation being an intensification of their suffering designed as part of their punishment.

There was real (and sadistic) theological muddle here, and the gruesomely punitive rationale for prayer for the dead which was dominant in the Middle Ages could be daunting, to say the least. There were always those uneasy with this account of things, and the greatest imaginative vision of the afterlife composed in the Middle Ages, Dante's *Commedia*, broke free from this suffocating gloom to offer a poetic vision of purgatory which relocated it more securely within the context of the gospel. For Dante too purgatory was a place; however, for him it was not a pit of despair, but a mountain of hope, reaching up into the light, and the sufferings there were designed to heal not to punish. All the pains of purgatory were imposed to reverse and undo the self-inflicted harms of sin, and the souls in purgatory eagerly embraced those pains as a therapy of love, '*solvendo il nodo*', dissolving the clenched knot of sin which held them back from God. The dominant colour in purgatory is green, the colour of hope and of renewal, and as Dante begins his ascent of the mountain of repentance after his traumatic descent into the pit of hell, Virgil, his guide, gently washes the tears and filth of sin from his face, foreshadowing the work of renewal which is the business of purgatory: in this place of hope, neither the living nor the dead have anything to fear.

By the end of the Middle Ages belief in purgatory had become one of the most vivid aspects of Catholicism, and prayer for the dead had become the chief activity of most clergy. In England, parish priests were outnumbered three to one by priests employed on fixed-term contracts singing Masses and reciting prayers for the repose of the souls of the more prosperous laity. One of medieval England's greatest poets, William Langland, was himself a lay clerk employed to recite psalms and prayers for the dead. The aisles and side-chapels of parish churches, monasteries and cathedrals were cluttered with altars to accommodate all these masses for the dead, and the churches were full of gifts – vestments, vessels, stained glass, elaborate images and monuments – all designed to evoke the gratitude of the congregations and to induce them to pray for the repose of the souls of the donors. Catholicism on the eve of the Reformation has been described, with pardonable exaggeration, as a religion of the living in the service of the dead.

The Protestant reformers swept all that away. None of this, they insisted, had any warrant in scripture (the account in 2 Maccabees of the sacrifices ordered by Judas Maccabeus for the dead came from the Apocrypha, which the reformers did not recognize as scripture). The whole idea of purgatory was rooted in Catholic understanding of penance, and this the reformers thought false, for it seemed to place salvation in human effort and voluntary human suffering. Purgatory was a bogey-man, a racket designed to keep the priests in luxury. Trust in God alone could save us. At death those with faith in the cross of Christ went straight to heaven, those without went straight to hell. And, as the English reformer Thomas Becon wrote, 'Heaven needeth no prayers, hell heedeth no prayers'. Prayer for the dead was presumptuous, and it was useless.

The reformers wanted to encourage Christians in a loving trust in God. But unintentionally they drove a wedge between the living and the dead: the saints did not pray for us, and we could do nothing for the dead. In effect, the dead were cut off from the great web of mutual love and support which was the Church. And in practice, the reformed doctrine struck the Church dumb at the graveside of sinners.

Reformed funeral rites, like that in the Book of Common Prayer, rejoiced that the Christian died 'in sure and certain hope of resurrection to eternal life'. But how could such confidence be spoken at the graveside of a murderer, a child abuser, an oppressor of the poor – or of the merely mediocre? There was a gulf in human experience between the hope which the gospel holds out for us all, and the reality of lives which even to those who loved them might seem imperfect and incomplete. Conscientious Protestant clergy, worried by the apparent lies they were required to utter when burying notorious sinners, selectively refused to speak the sentence about 'sure and certain hope' – and outraged relatives protested at this puritanical discrimination between the godly and the ungodly which seemed to damn their loved ones. With a larger charity and a deeper wisdom, the Catholic Church had from time immemorial insisted that at every graveside, whether of saint or sinner, we might say the same prayer – 'Lord have mercy'. In that prayer the Church expressed neither fear nor self-reliance, but faith and hope in the God who can bring meaning out of horror, and who loves even the unlovely.

For behind all the contradictory Catholic imaginings lay a piercing perception, that even for those who love God, death leaves unfinished business – damaged and damaging relationships, misunderstandings unresolved, words of love or apology or explanation unspoken, the need to forgive, and to be forgiven. What are we to do with such pain and incompleteness, but place it in the hands of God? In silencing prayer for the dead, the reformers left no space in prayer for these realities, and left Christians with no language except that of triumph in which to pray about the often far from triumphant experience of mortality.

Interestingly, despite the pervasiveness of punitive understandings of purgatory from the Middle Ages until comparatively recently, the Catholic Church allowed none of the accompanying technicolour horror any space inside her prayers for the dead. The prayers in the liturgy for the dead are often urgent in tone, pleas for salvation and deliverance in the face of death and the devil, but it would be impossible from those prayers alone to construct any specific picture of purgatory. Instead, they are filled with cries of supplication and hope for salvation, an extension into the realms of the dead of our faith and confidence in God, and our continuing love and concern for those who have died. So the essence of belief in purgatory was not the horror stories of the preachers and visionaries, but the conviction that even for those who died with their faith weak, their love imperfect, there might be healing at the hands of a loving redeemer. Prayer for the dead is neither fear nor fire insurance, emphatically not an attempt to appease an angry or sadistic God. It is an exercise in the virtues of faith and hope and love, even in the face of death, which puts an end to none of those things.

For prayer for the dead is also a bridge across the gulf of separation which is death. We are social beings, but most of us can expect to die alone, in a hospital bed rather than in our homes. Death is the ultimate alienation, the sacramental expression of all the barriers which divide us from one another. Medieval Christianity witnessed against that isolation by constantly remembering the dead, constantly recalling their names, in the liturgy and in private: the dead remained part of the community of the Church. The Church's faith is that in Christ the loneliness of death is overcome. Whatever the circumstances of our dying, the reality is that none of us dies alone, we are surrounded and supported by the prayers of the Church, a support which continues into the silence of death. The Reformation, in silencing all naming of the dead in prayer, unwittingly endorsed the experience of death as alienation: the dead were cast out of the company of the living, and the Church shrank to the living alone.

The reality of a shared life which transcends the grave, the solidarity of living and dead in Christ, is hard to hold on to, for

Catholics as well as for the churches of the Reformation. Elgar's *Dream of Gerontius*, that sublime setting of Newman's poem about the Christian soul in death and judgement, gives unforgettable expression to much that is noblest in Catholic belief about death and prayer for the dead. And Newman's understanding of purgatory is, on the face of it, very much that of Dante, a place of hope and healing, not of punishment. After judgement, the soul of Gerontius is gently immersed in the 'penal waters' of purgatory (no fire here), an obvious symbol of baptism, to await the day of deliverance. But there the resemblance between the purgatory of the *Commedia* and the purgatory of *Gerontius* ends. Dante's purgatory is a reflection of the solidarity and communality which for medieval Christendom was reflected in prayer for the dead: the souls being purged there move around in groups, talking to Dante and to one another, singing the hymns of the liturgy, supporting each other in their suffering, part of a single body of redeemed humanity. Newman, by contrast, was a romantic individualist, and his vision of purgatory is of an all but absolute loneliness. The angel lowers Gerontius into the lake, where he sinks alone, 'deep, deeper into the dim distance', and Gerontius sings,

> Take me away, and in the lowest deep there let me be
> And there in hope the lone night watches keep, told out
>   for me.
> There, motionless and happy in my pain, lone, not forlorn
> There will I sing my sad perpetual strain, until the morn.

It is true that Gerontius will be comforted in his suffering by 'masses on the earth and prayers in heaven', but these are imaginatively remote, noises offstage: the main drama is enacted between the lonely soul and its God. In this purgatory, the isolation of death remains the ultimate fact.

Images of purgatory come and go, some better than others, none of them essential. We do not pray for the dead to bail them out of prison or to placate a God who demands satisfaction, but because we know that they live in Christ, bound to us in a single faith and hope and love, and therefore with a right to a place in our prayers. We feel ourselves diminished by their deaths, and that has a reality in faith as well as in natural experience: bereavement is a religious as well as a natural fact. Salvation is complete for none until it is complete for all: the whole creation groans as it waits for redemption, and our prayers for the dead, like our belief that the saints pray for us, is a concrete expression of that conviction. In praying for the dead we pray also for ourselves, for we are only ourselves in relation to those who have shaped us and loved us, we are only ourselves in the company of our brothers and sisters. Praying for them, we put into words the pathos and the pain of our shared humanity. In the face of sin, ours and theirs, and confronted with the apparent waste, obscurity and isolation of death, we affirm our faith and hope in the God who creates us all, who loves us all and who wills to redeem us all.

(✓ Tom Wright's *recent* book on all this)
— Very *biblical* Nimme with the whole *business of* purgatory.

15

Hell

Over the west door of the Abbey Church at Conques is a great carving of the Last Judgement. Beneath the raised right arm of the enthroned Christ – does he bless or threaten? – cluster the saints, and the fortunate figures of the holy dead, rising to glory. To his left are the multitudes of the damned, dragged screaming from their graves by demons, crammed into the dragon mouth of hell, loaded with chains, stabbed with pitchforks, gnawed by monsters.

Christian art has rung the changes with endless ingenuity on hell, on all the details of divine retribution. Misers force-fed on molten gold, the lecherous suspended by their genitals, the justice of God depicted like the Mikado's 'object all sublime . . . to make the punishment fit the crime, the punishment fit the crime'. A sort of holy sadism has infected the Christian imagination confronted with the thought of damnation. One of the most popular British preachers of the nineteenth century was the aptly named Fr Furniss, a Redemptorist specializing in missions to children, who dwelt with lip-smacking relish on the tortures of the damned, 'every nerve trembling and quivering with sharp fire', flame raging through the skull, 'roaring in the throat as it roars up a chimney'. Cardinal Newman thought that most people would go to hell, 'like a herd of swine, falling headlong down the steep'. St Augustine thought that the contemplation of God's justice in the torments of the damned would be one of the joys of heaven.

They were made of sterner stuff than we are. No one

preaches hell-fire nowadays, for we prefer to think of God as far
too nice to damn anyone. A God of love will surely find room
in heaven for even the worst of us – it will all work out in the
end. And certainly, the God and Father of Our Lord Jesus
Christ everywhere reveals himself to us as one who wills that
everyone should be saved. He has only one word for us, and
that word is Love. *This is the essence of Evangelical antinomianism!*

Confidence in the love of God and his will to save all
whom he has made is the foundation of all faith. Any form of
Christianity which lets sin or hell loom larger than the loving
mercy of God in Christ is simply perverted. The trouble is
that the New Testament, above all Jesus himself, also insists on
the urgency and irrevocableness of the choices we make, on the
possibility of absolute loss, of spiritual and moral disaster. Here,
in this life, we become what we shall be in eternity. Christ
spoke of the few who enter the narrow gate of life, he evoked
the horror of final darkness, weeping and despair, and he used
the picture-language of the rubbish tip and the furnace to
describe the fate of those who made themselves incapable of
love, who failed to respond to the gospel.

To choose evil is to close ourselves to God, and this has
always been recognized by the theologians as the worst pain of
hell. Never to know the God by whom and for whom we have
been made, is to be alienated not only from him, but from our
own nature, our own kind. Unfortunately, our fallen nature is
such that we can contemplate such an alienation quite calmly, a
thick skin of indifference masks from us our incompleteness
without God. The thought of losing God should make our flesh
crawl, our souls turn sour. It mostly doesn't, however, and that
is why the tradition has piled on the agony, why the flames and
flesh-hooks have been imagined, to get across to us just how
devastating, how agonizing, such a loss would be.

If we are to make sense of this dimension of our tradition,
however, we need to grasp that language about hell is not
language about what *God* is capable of, but about what we
human beings are capable of. To believe in hell, to recognize
the possibility of damnation, is first and foremost to take

seriously the sort of world we live in, to grasp the need for choice. The century of Auschwitz and Belsen needs no picture language, no painting on a wall, to convince it of the reality and horror of evil, or of the likelihood that human beings might surrender themselves to evil until mercy, pity, peace shrivel within them. This is the world that crucified the Lord of Glory, utterly unregenerate, utterly alien from God. We trivialize the world's woes and betray the world's victims if we say glibly that everything will come right in the end, even for those who perpetrate such evil. Such magnanimity is for God, whose mercy is as deep as his justice. No human being is entitled to it, for in us such universal absolution is more likely to be born of indifference than of love.

To say all this, however, is not to pass final judgement on the perpetrators of evil. We cannot search the heart, and Judas himself may have repented at the end. But we can and must judge actions, because we must choose our sides. The concentration-camp commandant or the oppressor of the poor may be twisted, hapless beings, who deserve our pity more than our anger, if only all were known: but the oppression of the poor or the feeding of the gas chambers is devils' work. We need to be clear that it is damnable if we are to fight it, or more, if we are not to join in it ourselves.

For above everything, we believe in hell because we can imagine ourselves choosing it. We cannot know the secrets of other people's souls, but we know enough of our own to recognize something within us which shies away from God, something which wants to close our hearts to others. There is no inevitability about our response to God or to other people: hate and fear, as well as love and trust, are close to hand. Hell, in that sense, is a perpetual calling within us, from which only the loving mercy of God holds us back. We can trust in that mercy, but to trust in God's mercy is not the same as taking it for granted. We may hope for salvation for all humankind, even for ourselves: hell remains a terrible possibility, the dark side of our freedom.

But the last word in all this belongs not with our freedom,

Calvin said
Gethsemane was
hell.

but with God's grace. The most passionate modern theologian of hell was the late Hans Urs Von Balthasar, who returned to the possibility of damnation again and again in his writings. For Von Balthasar, Christ himself had descended on Good Friday into the heart of human desolation; Christ himself experienced damnation, as he entered the uttermost limits of humanity's alienation from God. Rejecting absolutely the easy optimism which denied the possibility of such loss for every human being, Von Balthasar nevertheless insisted that the essence of Christian hope was the prayer that hell might be utterly empty, that the mercy of God reached down even to those who willed damnation for themselves, plucking them despite themselves into the heart of love. Here, he wrote, 'lies hope for the person who, refusing all love, damns himself. Will not the man who wishes to be totally alone, find beside him in Sheol Someone lonelier still, the Son forsaken by the Father, who will prevent him from experiencing his self-chosen hell to the end?'

(This is
reminiscent
CS Lewis.

16

The Thinking Church:
A Recent History

The intellectual and spiritual history of English Catholics in the century and a half since the restoration of the hierarchy has had its giants – above all the towering figure of Cardinal Newman. But the ethos of the English Church has by and large militated against intellectual excellence and theological creativity. Victorian Catholicism, in the grip of the unprecedented social change of industrial England, and the influx of tens of thousands of impoverished Irish, was engaged in a massive work of stabilization and basic education. But in the century after 1850 Catholic education meant, in England and Wales, essentially one thing and one thing only: the creation of a primary and secondary school system controlled by Catholics themselves, essentially by the clergy, in which the faith could be transmitted to the community's children. From 1867 Catholics were forbidden to study at Oxford and Cambridge, and despite abortive aspirations by Cardinal Manning for a Catholic University, priorities in tertiary education were much lower, and (in the form of teacher training colleges and seminaries) mainly designed to service the schools and parishes. The schools question dominated the community's financial preoccupations and the policy-making of the hierarchy. Cardinal Manning, famously, would not build a cathedral for the Westminster archdiocese until every Catholic child had a place in a Catholic school. Ireland apart, insofar as there has been a coherent Catholic politics in Britain over the last 150 years, it has been the politics of the schools question.

It was an issue which increasingly defined Catholic identity. The standard Catholic Catechism in 1859 asked, 'What is the duty of parents and other superiors?', and answered, 'To take proper care of all under their charge, and to bring up their children in the fear of God.' By the 1880s, that had become 'The duty of parents towards their children is to provide for them, to instruct and correct them, and to give them a good Catholic education.' The same Catechism went on to warn that 'We expose ourselves to the danger of losing our Faith by neglecting our spiritual duties, reading bad books, *going to non-Catholic schools*, and taking part in services or prayers of a false religion.'

The result, on the debit side, was a community isolated from the main intellectual trends of the nation at large and which, though producing many figures of distinction, particularly from the major religious orders, was essentially without any sustained or consistently promoted intellectual culture. Above all, among English Catholics theology was rarely studied in order to unfold or deepen understanding of the mystery of faith, but was conceived of essentially as a branch of apologetics.

That is not to say that the community was, by its own standards, unsuccessful. The heroic struggle for the schools did succeed in creating a distinctive Catholic ethos, which, though increasingly storm-beleaguered, has persisted almost to the present. David Lodge's *How Far Can You Go?* published in 1980, is the most painfully funny evocation of what it was like to be a young university-educated Catholic in Britain in the 1960s and 1970s. It opens with an early-morning Mass set in the gaunt London church of our Lady and St Jude (hopeless causes, a nice touch!) on St Valentine's Day 1952, attended by the group of London University students who will form the *dramatis personae* of the book. Most of them are the products of intensely Catholic backgrounds, soaked in and acquiescent to the minutiae of Catholic teaching and sub-cultural peculiarity (hinted at in the depressing grey drizzle through which they have struggled to Mass), and the opening pages of the novel read like a crash course in some of the more exotic features of

Catholicism as then understood – in half a chapter we are
introduced to transubstantiation, holidays of obligation, works
of supererogation, the difference between mortal and venial sin,
the Rosary, plenary indulgences, purgatory, and the almost
permanently tormented state of a pubescent young Catholic
male's conscience.

The novel culminates a generation later with the televising of
an experimental mid-1970s Easter Vigil, organized by a group
called COC ('Catholics for an Open Church') in which white-
robed charismatic nuns dance on a college playing field as the
sun rises, a Latin American theologian in a combat jacket
preaches revolution, and a voice-over by a well-meaning but
slightly bewildered young priest, soon to leave the priesthood
for a PhD in sociology, and marriage to a secretary, expresses
doubts about the resurrection. An anonymous commentator – is
it Lodge himself? – sums up the changes which the book has
chronicled.

> Many things have changed – attitudes to authority, sex,
> worship, other Christians, other religions. But perhaps the
> most fundamental change is one that the majority of
> Catholics themselves are scarcely conscious of. It's the
> fading away of the traditional Catholic metaphysic – that
> marvellously complex and ingenious synthesis of theology
> and cosmology and casuistry, which situated individual
> souls on a kind of spiritual Snakes and Ladders board,
> motivated them with equal doses of hope and fear, and
> promised them, if they persevered in the game, an eternal
> reward. The board was marked out very clearly, decorated
> with all kinds of picturesque motifs, and governed by
> intricate rules and provisos. Heaven, Hell, Purgatory,
> Limbo. Mortal venial and original sin. Angels, devils,
> saints, and Our Lady Queen of Heaven. Grace, penance,
> relics, indulgences and all the rest of it. Millions of
> Catholics no doubt still believe in all that literally. But
> belief is gradually fading. That metaphysic is no longer
> taught in schools and seminaries in the more advanced

countries, and Catholic children are growing up knowing little or nothing about it. Within another generation or two it will have disappeared, superseded by something less vivid but more tolerant.

How Far Can You Go? is of course fiction, but its analysis of the psychological, social and intellectual upheavals which underlie the comic dilemmas of Lodge's characters, caught in the flux of modernity and the dissolution of inherited Catholic certainties, is very shrewd, and still touches a nerve. Lodge's point, returned to in a number of his books, is that the Catholic metaphysic was inseparable from the tight web of Catholic practice. Apparently timeless certainties, the 'Faith of our Fathers' dimension of Catholicism, had actually turned out to be part of a package deal, wound into and in part dependent for credibility on a set of cultural practices and attitudes which have now gone or are going as irrevocably as the demise of the dinosaurs. This Catholic culture was vivid, and often endearing – it is evoked in the football scores of the Catholic youth clubs in South London in the 1950s in another of Lodge's novels, *Therapy* – 'Immaculate Conception 2, Precious Blood 1 . . . Perpetual Succour 3, Forty Martyrs, nil', but it was part of the life of a community whose history of disadvantage and discrimination, and whose strong (almost 50 per cent) first-, second- or third-generation Irish component, combined to gave it a distinctive and strongly defined sense of separate identity. In Lodge's admittedly highly coloured portrayal, Catholicism on the eve of the Council was not a set of opinions one adopted, it was a community and a way of life one signed up for: and it was the work of Catholic education not to question or complicate, but to transmit this way of life.

But it was a way of life which, though it seemed immemorial, was actually a cultural construct, the product of a network of specific circumstances. In the 1950s, a century on from the re-establishment of the hierarchy, it was a community on the crest of a wave of self-confidence and success. The Catholic Church throughout Britain was one of the principal beneficiaries of the Butler Education Act of 1944. In the 25 years after the Second World War, Catholic schools would be transformed, and a swelling wave of pupils from the Catholic schools would flood on into the universities. The community itself was growing, the estimated Catholic population of England and Wales moving rapidly towards four million, baptisms topping 100,000 a year, adult conversions touching 15,000. The seminaries and religious orders were packed, and ambitious new building programmes were adopted to accommodate the boom.

Yet despite all that, the English Catholic Church was by and large intellectually ill-prepared for the Council. Its leaders were practical men, whose intellectual culture was culled from second-rate Roman textbooks, for whom theology was a bore, and for whom liturgy was rubrics, something one memorized from the pages of manuals like Fortescue-O'Connell, *The Ceremonies of the Roman Rite Described*. With a few notable exceptions, the imaginative level of the hierarchy of the first half of the century was best indicated by a famous remark of Cardinal Bourne, Archbishop of Westminster in the 1920s, who declared that, 'I never start anything, but I never stop anything.' In England during the Second Vatican Council, the Cardinal Archbishop of Westminster, John Carmel Heenan, was fairly representative – an able man and a charismatic pastor, but on his own admission someone who 'had never had a serious doubt in his life'. He was temperamentally and intellectually ill-equipped to steer the community through the theological white-water of the 1960s and early 1970s.

The Council profoundly changed the orientation of Catholic theology, ecclesiology and spirituality in a number of ways. The whole tone of its documents, and the fundamental decision to produce no new definitions or anathemas, was in itself a decisive break with what one may call the tradition of the Vatican Jeremiad. This was the spirit of confrontation, the repudiation of non-ecclesial culture, which had characterized the public utterance of the Church for more than a century and which is summed up in documents like the *Syllabus of Errors* of 1864, in which the teaching office of the Church is understood primarily in terms of the condemnation of error, rather than the positive encouragement of truth. The shift to the vernacular in worship reintroduced into Catholic liturgical and devotional experience a decisive element of regional variety which was bound to have theological as well as pastoral implications, however carefully policed it might be.

The Conciliar process itself – the meetings between the bishops of the world, and between their theologians, the sense of the shared labour of the whole Church and not simply the central organs of the papacy to discern and proclaim the Catholic faith which comes to us from the apostles, the public experience of the whole Church, pastors and people, engaged together in learning and in changing – all this decisively and permanently shifted Catholic perception of the nature of the Church, and the role of the *magisterium* within it.

The Council then, left us with a very different sort of Church, far more responsive to lay expectation, far more theologically alert and diverse. Yet there were and are those who believed that this amazing and Spirit-led experience should have produced a far greater and more decisive conversion of hearts, minds and structures, a root-and-branch rebirth of the Church in a 'New Pentecost'. If the Church was more responsive to lay expectation, that lay expectation was itself growing, and a great deal more vocal. When, not very surprisingly, a heavily clerical and authoritarian institution, its clericalism embedded in the code of Canon Law, failed to transform itself at once into a place of dialogue and partnership between laity and priesthood, sharp disillusion set in. In England that disappointment found a particular focus in the aftermath of the Liverpool Pastoral Congress of 1980, and the Episcopal response, *The Easter People*. The sense of the failure of the years since the Council to deliver their promise – 'Whatever Happened to Vatican II?' – has persisted among many of those old enough to have shared in the initial euphoria of reform in the white heat of the Conciliar years themselves; and something of this sense, for example, characterized many of

His writings are significant & readable

the papers delivered at the symposium on the Catholic Church and the New Millennium organized a few of years ago at the University of Surrey by Michael Hornsby Smith.

One prominent and persistent theme of the liberal critique of the present state of the Church has been its failure adequately to absorb the characteristic values and institutions of democracy – dialogue, consultation, accountability. The pressure for greater involvement of women – and maybe their eventual ordination – derives some of its force from 'democratic' rather than strictly theological arguments. Yet for many, this process of accommodation has gone disastrously too far. The Catholic Church in this country is now far more at ease in the culture than it was on the eve of the Council: Catholics are to be found at every level of English life, a visible Catholic presence is mandatory at all solemn state occasions, and the once all-pervasive cultural anti-Catholicism has receded – all of this a process materially assisted by the personality and gifts of the late Cardinal Hume.

Yet there are many who view this *rapprochement* with the establishment with dismay. In *The Two Catholic Churches: A Study in Oppression*, a powerful and controversial book published in 1986, the (then) Dominican Antony Archer suggested that the transformations of the Church in England after Vatican Two were a betrayal of the working class to whom on the eve of the Council the Catholic Church had unique and privileged access. The advent of a vernacular liturgy and forms of Christian involvement which placed a premium on discussion and activism had, he thought, merely taken control of the Church away from the clergy and handed it to the chattering classes, who had every interest in making the Catholic Church as much like the Church of England as possible – and that, with the co-operation of a newly professionalized clergy, was what Archer thought had happened. The Church had opted for power, acceptability and talk, and in the process had abandoned its proper constituency among the powerless and inarticulate.

Archer's attack on the actual outcome of the Conciliar reforms in England was launched from the left: he was not opposed to change, but disliked the form the change had taken. On the right, there were those who, quite simply, thought the faith had been betrayed, that ecumenism and doctrinal deviation were the poisoned fruits of liturgical change, and that the Council, if not the cause, was at least the occasion for a disastrous collapse of Catholic value, which had to be reversed. This point of view was less fiercely and divisively expressed in England than elsewhere, but their case drew strength from the fact that in the years since the Council, the English Church's post-war boom has been steadily evaporating. Though the nominal Catholic population continued to grow, the real indicators of Catholic practice began a downward spiral in the early 1970s, which has continued and grown steeper, bringing the Church in England into line with the Catholic Church elsewhere in Europe. In the immediate aftermath of the Council, in England as everywhere else in the West, there was an exodus from the priesthood and (especially) the religious orders, and recruitment to the seminaries dipped. In 1968 there were almost 5,000 secular priests in England and Wales, and 2,762 ordained male religious. 1998 statistics indicate just over 4,000 secular priests and 1,682 religious, with the age-profile of serving priests steadily worsening: cobwebs gather in the corridors of the seminary extensions of the early 1960s. Perhaps more significantly, Mass attendance has declined: the latest figures are just over 1,100,000 each week, not much more than a quarter of the estimated Catholic population, while baptisms have shrunk to 67,000 a year, and marriages have declined to 15,500, very much less than half the 1958 figure. Once-flourishing Catholic organizations like the Children of Mary or the Union of Catholic Mothers have nose-dived, and the religious orders, especially the active or 'Apostolic' orders founded in the eighteenth and nineteenth centuries, have been decimated.

But if many of the institutions of the English Church are in decline, the educational level of Catholics themselves has never been higher. The dramatic transformation of the social and intellectual standing of the laity demands a comparable transformation of the structures of involvement within the institutional

Church. Specifically, the priest is now by no means always or even often the best educated person in a local congregation. In many places this is true even in the area of theology, for one feature of the educational transformation of the Catholic community since the 1960s has been the very large number of men and women seeking some form of tertiary theological education. Despite the lack of a Catholic University, there is now for the first time in England an emergent Catholic theological culture which, partly because of that very lack, is unlike anything to be found in Europe or America. Though theology is taught to a variety of levels and in a variety of styles in Catholic institutions, such as Heythrop College or Trinity and All Saints Leeds or the Maryvale Institute, many Catholics study their theology in specifically ecumenical contexts, and Catholics are a major presence both as teachers and students in university faculties and departments of theology or religious studies. The meaning of 'Catholic theology' given such diversity is a complicated matter, and given the plurality of providers of such education, coherence can no longer be equated with or derived from tight hierarchical control of curricula or standards. This is a relatively new situation, in which the 'Catholicism' of theology is to be found in the ecclesial allegiance and orientation of the practitioner rather than in a single specifically 'Catholic' agenda, style or content of theological practice.

There are huge questions here about what exactly constitutes the essence of Catholicism, and how, in a world as diverse and pluralistic as ours, the spiritual coherence of Catholicism can be sustained and nourished without intellectual aridity or coercion. We cannot and should not now try to reconstruct or recapture Lodge's 'Catholic metaphysic', for it was not in fact the distillation of eternal truths, but the product of a unique sub-culture, a moment (admittedly pretty extended) of cultural containment and uniformity that has now almost certainly passed for ever. My own conviction is that the root of that matter must now lie in the coherence and depth of the liturgical life of the community, and this is an area in which I fear we are in serious trouble, because of the the systematic ritual decentring of

Catholicism which was often promoted in the name of *aggiornamento* in the wake of the Council.

That is an issue for another essay altogether, but if the incipient theological energy and diversity within the English Catholic community is to nourish rather than confuse, it needs this sort of ecclesial 'centring' or focus: what will in the end secure the Catholicity of our theology is not its confinement to a check-list of Catholic truths or methods, but its practice within and for the Church. That can be ensured in a number of ways – by the increasing employment of appropriately trained men and women in theological work for the Church at parish and diocesan as well as national level, by the provision and encouragement of contexts for theological exchange such as those offered by organizations like the Catholic Theological Association, and by the systematic promotion of theological exchange in conferences and the press.

There are as yet few signs that the institutional Church in England takes really seriously the specifically intellectual challenge of theology. This is a deep-seated lack. English bishops have been for the most part pragmatists and practical men. Few have had active theological interests, and, in contrast to the situation in France or Germany, no English Catholic bishop since St John Fisher has written a work of lasting theological value. The English hierarchy, for understandable reasons, has tended to value the practical works of mercy and justice as the real test of Christian effectiveness. That is perhaps as it should be, but if the years since the Council have taught us anything, it must surely be that if Christian action is to remain Christian, it needs to be based in reflection on the Christian mystery, it needs a deep theological root.

The tending of that root is the proper responsibility of bishops, whom the canon of the Mass actually describes as *cultores* – 'gardeners' or 'husbandmen' – of the Catholic faith. The bishops in the century after the establishment of the hierarchy laboured heroically to provide a basic Catholic education for the community's children. It would be a worthwhile challenge for their successors in the coming century to seek – and be seen to seek – the theological education of the whole community.

Note: This essay incorporates material from the 2000 Meyer Lectures at Mundelein Seminary in the Archdiocese of Chicago.

17

Scandal in the Church:
Some Bearings from History

Scandals are rocking the Church throughout the Western world, successive and apparently endless revelations of clerical sexual misdemeanour, above all the abuse of children. In Ireland until recently a distinctively puritanical style of Catholicism policed and discouraged lay sexual freedoms, like contraception and divorce, taken for granted everywhere else. The discovery that the institution which preached these austerities not only harboured but is alleged to have protected sexually predatory priests and religious, who have betrayed the trust placed in them, and inflicted immeasurable harm on those they have abused, has contributed to a widespread withdrawal of confidence in what had seemed an unshakeable pillar of Irish identity. Congregations have thinned, media coverage is cynically hostile, and vocations, already under pressure, have largely collapsed. In Ireland, as in America and to a lesser extent in Britain and in Europe, it is a bad time to be a Catholic priest, and many feel that it is a bad time to be a Catholic.

There is no softening the horror of sexual abuse, and it is paedophilia rather than simple sexual misdemeanour which gives all this its devastating effect. The former Bishop of Galway's long-term affair, in the course of which he fathered an illegitimate son, now seems a mild and reassuring peccadillo, compared with the gross exploitation of children and the vulnerable which are the stuff of the current wave of scandals. These are betrayals of a particularly revolting kind, and they are deservedly being hunted out in the full blaze of twenty-first-century publicity. There has never been anything quite like this before, and it is hard to predict its long-term effect on the place of the Catholic Church in public life. Certainly much of the publicity comes from sources already hostile to Christianity, and eager for ammunition against it, and our society anyway is informed by a sort of hectic glee at the discrediting of virtue, the defiling of the holy: we love to be told that nothing is sacred. But it would be self-deception to imagine that all this is being whipped up from outside. These multiple betrayals reveal something badly amiss in the Church itself; they are a call to fundamental reappraisal and penitence, rather than to a closing of ranks.

But if these sorts of revelations are comparatively new, ecclesiastical abuse itself is not. The current scandals derive their power to shock and disorientate because for the last three or four centuries we have come to expect — and to assume that we get — the highest standards from clergy. There is nothing inevitable about such an expectation, and when it first appeared in the sixteenth century, it represented a revolutionary break with the past. Since the Council of Trent the official ideal of priestly formation underlying the training of clergy has been a very exalted one, emphasizing holiness of life and the separation of the priest from the contaminating influences of secular life. Clergy were to be recruited young, and separated from family and locality in special 'seminaries' or 'seed-beds' where, under the supervision of older priests, they lived a disciplined communal life designed to inculcate a distinctive clerical identity and an exalted set of spiritual values, focused especially on rigorous sexual abstinence.

The Tridentine ideal represented a revolutionary new departure in the training of clergy because up until then priests had mostly been recruited from village altar boys and trained by a system of apprenticeship, often to a priest-relative who might well be the boy's own father. And although it was legislated for at Trent, in reality the process of the separation of priests from the secular world took centuries to realize — Pope Benedict XIV was still struggling to introduce seminaries for the first time into the impoverished bishoprics of southern Italy in the mid-eighteenth century. However, the seminary revolution was achieved everywhere in Europe by the mid-nineteenth century, and our current perceptions of priesthood, and the high moral and spiritual expectations we place on our priests, are a product of that revolution. At its most demanding, it is an heroic ideal, in which the priest's celibacy and spiritual loneliness is understood as a profound *imitatio Christi*, a suffering ministry undertaken on behalf of his people. It was given exemplary embodiment in the life of the Cure D'Ars, and unforgettable literary expression in George Bernanos' *Diary of a Country Priest*.

The pervasiveness of that ideal by the nineteenth century meant that clerical sin became profoundly shocking, almost literally unthinkable. More than at any previous time in the history of the Church, it became an unspoken assumption that a priest, a bishop, a pope, must be, should be, a saint. By contrast, medieval Christians expected their clergy to be sinful, and were accustomed to moral and spiritual compromises which the post-Tridentine Church would come to consider outrageous. Clerical concubinage, for example, was extremely common in the Middle Ages, and the great Dutch humanist scholar Erasmus of Rotterdam was the bastard son of a concubinate priest. Clerical marriage and concubinage had been routine in the first millennium, not least in Britain: almost all the secular clergy referred to in the twelfth-century *Life of St William of Norwich* were married men. The marriage of priests was outlawed by reforming popes from the late eleventh century onwards, but although this official disapproval came to be widely accepted, and the laity increasingly preferred their priests to be celibate, there was a widespread acceptance of the gulf between ideal and actuality.

In many places clerical concubinage was accepted as a form of common-law marriage, and some communities even made their priests sign contracts undertaking not to take a concubine from the village, but to find their woman elsewhere, so as not to deplete the local stock of marriageable girls. And in some parts of Europe, even monks were not exempt from the general slackness of sexual attitude. In southern Italy one fifteenth-century bishop inspecting a local monastery discovered the abbot surrounded by children and harbouring a wife in his cell. When ordered to banish his family, the abbot protested that he doted on the children, and besides, his doctor had prescribed regular sexual intercourse as a remedy for his gall-stones. Medieval Christians of course disapproved of such flagrant abuses, but they were not surprised by them, and they took them in their stride as a recurrent feature of life in the Church: the satirical works of even so devout a Catholic as Thomas More are filled with just such stories. And the awareness of failure went right to the top. Christians of More's generation were hardened to the spectacle of popes presiding at the baptism of their children or grandchildren in the Vatican; or equally disturbingly, of popes clad in armour leading armies into murderous battles against their spiritual children.

Paradoxically, one major consequence of the hardening of Western Christian hostility to clerical marriage in the Middle Ages was that medieval people were forced to come to terms with the knowledge that because of the ban, many, in some places most, of their clergy were 'living in sin'. St Francis of Assisi repeatedly insisted that his friars should treat the local parish clergy with respect because of their ordination, even though this meant turning a blind eye to the priest's sinful life: they should kiss the priest's hand even if they knew it was the hand of a sexual sinner. The first work of spiritual direction for the laity written in English, the early thirteenth-century *Ancrenne Wisse*, warned the women hermits for whom it was intended against contact with secular priests or monks of the old orders. The assumption of the writer was that priests and monks would have no wisdom worth offering to holy women, and, more to the point, that they could not be trusted alone with them. Instead, the women should accept spiritual direction only from the Friars, who had recently arrived in England and whose exemplary lives of poverty and purity were widely admired.

Notoriously, however, the fresh bloom soon came off the

Mendicant ideal, too. Dominant in the universities, and increasingly conformed to the patterns of the older religious orders, the radical simplicity and austerity of the early Friars Minor and Friars Preacher soon gave way to establishment status. From about 1270 onwards the buildings of the Franciscans in England had become increasingly grandiose. The London Greyfriars begun in 1279 was 300 feet long, 89 feet wide and 64 feet high: among the burials of the great and the good which thronged its floors in the thirteenth and fourteenth centuries (and which would continue unabated till the house was dissolved under Henry VIII) were the remains and monuments not only of grandees of the City Companies and former Lord Mayors, but of a bevy of earls and duchesses, the heart of a queen of England, and the body of a queen of Scotland. So the poet William Langland complained that:

> . . . friars followed folk that was rich
> And folk that was poor at little price they set,
> And no corpse in their kirkyard nor in their kirk was
>   buryed
> But quick [unless while alive] he bequethed them aught or
>   should help pay their debts.

In a devastating commentary on the erosion of the Franciscan ideal of poverty, the London house of Greyfriars was robbed in 1355 by one of its own members: his loot included gold, silver and jewels worth £200, an immense sum in contemporary terms.

Langland's *Vision of Piers Plowman*, a product of the age of Chaucer and Richard II, gives voice to a lay Christianity often at odds with the clerical establishment, deeply disillusioned by the huge distance between the Church's vocation to holiness and the sordid actuality. Langland returns again and again to the value of a simple faith enacted in charity, not in empty profession. The poem is informed by anger at the ills of the contemporary Church, seen as compromised by slackness and corruption from top to bottom – 'Unkonnynge [ignorant] curates', who lead their parishioners to perdition, worldly prelates motivated by pride and greed, 'heremits on a heap' wending to Walsingham 'and their wenches after', above all the friars, covetous deceivers, peddling cheap grace to eager hearers, and dumbing down the demands of the gospel in order to line their own pockets

> . . . all the four orders
> Preached to the people for profit of themselves,
> Glossed the Gospel as they good liked
> For covetous of copes, construed it as they would.

Our generation of Christians has been horrified by revelations of clerical sexual hypocrisy and abuse. As these examples suggest, however, clerical greed shocked medieval Christians at least as much as clerical lust, and they were deeply scandalized by the 'unnatural' marriage between religious life and financial greed, the racketeering which posed as piety. Covetousness was central to Langland's powerful and pessimistic analysis of the state of the fourteenth-century Church: he targeted clerical greed as one of the root evils of Christendom. He believed this greed would rot society to the core and he looked to the secular arm, to king and parliament, for remedies: as Conscience declares:

> Sir king, by Christ, unless clerks amend
> Thy kingdom through their covetousness will out of
> nature wend,
> And holy church through them be harmed for ever.

This sort of pessimism about the lives of the clergy was not confined to England, of course, where indeed clerical standards seem to have been as high as anywhere in Europe. The circles of Dante's hell are thronged with wicked priests, bishops and popes: interestingly, it is seldom sex which has sent them there. For Dante as for other medieval Christians, there were much worse sins than fornication – envy, pride, murder. One of the most terrible scenes in that most terrible of books is Dante's encounter in the lowest circle of hell with the traitor Ugolino, eternally gnawing the living skull of Archbishop Ruggieri of Pisa, who had walled him and his sons up in a tower and left them to starve. Dante detests, but he is not surprised by, the mortal sins of even the most exalted priests of the Church.

Before the modern era, then, Christians were familiar with and outspoken about scandal in the Church. That doesn't of course mean that they did not want to reform it: Langland and Dante in their different ways sought to challenge and change the Church by what they wrote; they looked for renewal and purification. And their world was different from ours, because they lived in societies which were overwhelmingly Christian, where alternative world-views like Islam or Judaism were controlled minorities or external enemies. For them Church and world overlapped and interlinked, in a way which we can barely imagine, and the reform of society inevitably involved the purification of the Church. Reformers therefore freely named and shamed the evils of the Church, which affected everyone.

Since the sixteenth century, however, and especially since the end of the eighteenth century, the Church has operated increasingly at the margins of society, has felt itself to be not the spiritual dimension of society as a whole but an alternative society, often beleagured, always in need of defence. One consequence of the spread of exalted clerical standards and expectations was an undoubted rising of the standards of the priesthood: the rank and file clergy of 1900 were immeasurably better educated and better behaved than their counterparts of 1500 or 1600. But a less desirable spin-off has been the emergence alongside this raising of standards of a culture of denial, a concern to protect the Church's good name, sometimes at all costs. This has often been maintained by a sort of collusive fiction in which clergy and laity alike have averted their eyes from the realities of human frailty within the institution.

That condition has often gone along with an authoritarian

mind-set which insists that 'we never make mistakes', and which interprets criticism as disloyalty. But the problem is much deeper than any straightforward pulling of clerical rank, or the desire of a caste to defend its turf. The practical ecclesiology of the medieval Church was profoundly Augustinian, preaching holiness but expecting Christians, including the clergy, in practice to be sinners, the institution itself a 'hospital for incurables' as much as a school of perfection.

But for several centuries our practical ecclesiology has been Donatist rather than Augustinian, emphasizing the perfections of the Church and its ministers, unable to accommodate or to admit failure. This phenomenon was undoubtedly nourished by clerical Ultramontanism, but it is important to register that it was not confined to the Church. The emergence of the professions in modern England involved until relatively recently rather similar assumptions about the infallibility and impeccability of doctors, teachers, policemen and civil servants: the respectability of priests went alongside the assumed respectability of other professionals. For good or ill, we are all more suspicious now.

There is no obvious moral, certainly no obvious remedy for our current ills, to be deduced from these forays into history, though some commentators have been quick to offer such morals. To some, it is clear that the thousand-year-old experiment with the enforced celibacy of the secular clergy has failed, and the way forward lies in a married priesthood, better integrated into the lay society in which their parishioners have to live out their Christianity.

For others, the remedy is diametrically opposed, and lies in a stern reaffirmation of the Tridentine ideal after the slackness of the 'silly season', when sexual permissiveness and theological confusion invaded the Church and rotted its values, in the pontificate of Paul VI. On this analysis we need stricter seminaries, and zealous priests more rigorously separated by lifestyle, dress and intellectual formation from the secular world and its values.

Neither conclusion strikes me as obvious: if the recent wave of paedophile arrests of celebrities is anything to go by, celibacy is not at the root of that particular ill. Equally however, the tightening of the Tridentine ideal and the barricading of men into sixteenth- or nineteenth-century clericalist styles and role models seems likely to breed just that state of fantasy and denial which has enabled some priests and religious to live lives of such baffling and shocking duplicity. If history offers no obvious solutions, however, it does at least provide the comfort of knowing that failure is nothing new. Earlier generations of Christians have understood more deeply and acknowledged more frankly that the treasure of the gospel is held in earthen vessels.

18

What About the Inquisition?

The Inquisition was one of the best reasons the Victorians could think of to loathe and distrust the Catholic Church. Tennyson's rousing patriotic poem 'The Revenge, a Ballad of the Fleet', tells the story of the heroic stand against overwhelming odds by the Elizabethan sailor Sir Richard Grenville. Outnumbered by more than 50 ships to one, Grenville cannot flee, since, as he tells the English Admiral, he had:

> ninety men and more who are lying sick ashore
> he will not abandon them:
> to these Inquisition dogs and the devildoms of Spain.
> The sick men are brought aboard:
> and they blessed him in their pain that they were not left
> to Spain
> To the thumbscrew and the stake for the glory of the Lord.

Modern Catholic sensibility too revolts against the idea of 'the thumbscrew and the stake' being employed 'for the glory the Lord'. Yet for more than a millennium the Catholic Church thought it right to combat heresy and enforce orthodoxy and Catholic morality by the use of force, including the death penalty. Some such development was probably almost inevitable once Christianity became the official religion of the Roman Empire, and as early as the fifth century St Augustine himself had justified the forcible conversion of Donatist schismatics by a strained and unnatural interpretation of the

phrase 'compel them to come in' from the Gospel parable of
the wedding feast.

Where Augustine led, others followed: forced conversions of whole populations were routine aspects of the Christianization of Europe in the early Middle Ages. The Inquisition itself, however, took another seven centuries to appear. At the beginning of the twelfth century a frightening heresy was spreading through southern and western Europe. Known as 'Catharism' (from the Greek word for purity) it was a dualistic religion which denied the value of the material world, and it therefore seemed to undermine not only the whole sacramental system of the Church, but the fundamental institutions of Christian society, especially marriage. The normal episcopal machinery for searching out and restraining heresy was ineffective against Catharism, which recognized no diocesan boundaries, and whose teachers travelled freely through northern Spain, Southern France, Northern Italy, and even further afield. Starting with Innocent III, a series of popes set in place an international commission of enquiry with extensive powers of arrest and judgement.

This papal 'Inquisition', formally established in 1233 by Pope Gregory IX, was staffed mostly by Dominican and Franciscan friars, and it came to be greatly feared. Inquisitors were answerable to the pope alone: they could arrest suspects on the testimony of two witnesses (who remained anonymous), and from 1252 they had papal licence to use torture to extract information. A formidable body of case law was built up and formulated into Inquisitors' manuals, to consolidate the experience and the record-keeping of the Inquisitors. Suspects or witnesses were compelled to give evidence under threat of heavy penalties, and assisting a heretic became a grave crime, making lawyers reluctant to act as counsel for the defence in case suspicion fell on them. Suspects found guilty of heresy had ecclesiastical penances imposed on them, which might include the wearing of a badge of shame. Stubborn or relapsed heretics were 'relaxed' to the secular authorities, for execution as a danger to Christian society. The normal form of such execution, established by the Emperor Frederick II in Sicily, was burning alive.

The medieval Inquisition established itself through most of medieval Europe, from Scandinavia to Southern Spain, though never, interestingly, in England. An attempt to introduce Inquisitors here was made in 1309, as part of the campaign against the Knights Templar. The attempt foundered, because the English clergy and laity distrusted a legal process that did not follow the English form of trial by jury, involved anonymous testimony, and required the use of sanctified violence against suspects. The two French inquisitors sent to conduct proceedings against the Templars complained bitterly of the lack of qualified torturers in England, and returned, disgusted, to France.

Heresy was not the only target of the Inquisitors. Any offence against the faith might fall under the Inquisition's remit, and in the fifteenth century the most lurid of these offences was thought to be witchcraft. In December 1484 Pope Innocent VIII issued a disastrous Bull, *Summis Desiderantes*, designed to further the witch-hunting activities of the Inquisition in Germany. In the Bull, Pope Innocent endorsed the grotesque idea that men and women formed sexual partnerships with demons, and he took at face value the whole gamut of contemporary superstition about witches. The Bull had been secured by the two leading anti-witch Inquisitors in Germany, Heinrich Kramer and Jacob Sprenger: in its wake, they produced the most notorious of all Inquisitors' manuals, the *Malleus Malificarum* (hammer of the Witches) which was to play an enormous and vicious role in spreading belief in the existence of demonic witchcraft. In the process, it contributed to the deaths of countless thousands of harmless or eccentric women over the next 300 years. In all, as many as 25,000 people, most of them women, may have been burned as witches in Germany. By no means all or even most of these were tried by the Inquisition, but the official backing of pope and Inquisition for witch beliefs certainly contributed to the credibility and spread of witch-hunting.

Witches

In Spain, the Inquisition took a very distinctive shape. Early medieval Spain had sheltered Christian, Muslim and Jewish populations in a remarkable religious coexistence. By the end of the Middle Ages that earlier pluralism, always fragile, had collapsed, the Muslim areas of the peninsula had been conquered, and the Spanish monarchy was intent on eliminating Judaism and Islam altogether. A key tool in this campaign was the Spanish Inquisition, established at the request of the Crown by the Spanish Pope Sixtus IV (Borja) in 1478. The Spanish Inquisition was directly subject to the Spanish Monarchy, not the papacy, and it was from the first an instrument of racial and ethnic cleansing, hunting out any hint that former Jews and Muslims were secretly practising their old faith: a dislike of pork or the habit of changing your underwear on Saturday might be taken as damning – and potentially fatal – evidence of this sort of relapse.

The Spanish Inquisition's enormous powers and strong-arm methods earned it a fearsome reputation, and when Europe split into Protestant and Catholic camps in the sixteenth century, the Spanish Inquisition in particular would come to be seen as the unacceptable face of militant Catholicism, torturing and burning Protestants, and keeping the Catholic population also in submission. The reputation would persist, and was to receive its greatest literary expression in the nineteenth century, long after the Inquisition itself had ceased to exist, in Dostoevsky's fable of the Grand Inquisitor, in *The Brothers Karamazov*. In that fable, Christ returns to earth in late medieval Spain, but is arrested and confronted by the Grand Inquisitor Torquemada, who rejects Christ because he will upset the Church's control over the minds and hearts of mankind, who would rather not think, suffer or hope for themselves: 'Why have you come to disturb us?' *(a marvellous tale)*

Outside the Iberian peninsula, however, the medieval Inquisitions had declined to insignificance by the time of the Reformation. To remedy this decline and to meet the challenge of militant Protestantism, the Roman Inquisition was established in 1542 under Pope Paul III, to centralize the struggle against error in Europe and the wider world. Successive sixteenth-century popes strengthened it: a special curial congregation was established to oversee its work (the direct ancestor of the present Congregation for the Doctrine of the Faith), and another congregation was founded to control the censorship of books – the Congregation of the Index. By the sixteenth century, however, even Catholic states were wary of an international papal tribunal with powers which overrode local customs. Though the Roman Inquisition played a part in the struggle against the Reformation all over Catholic Europe, it was often carefully controlled by the secular power. In the devoutly Catholic state of Venice, for example, the Inquisitors always sat alongside secular magistrates appointed by the government, and proceedings against prominent citizens of the Republic were often hampered or aborted.

The Roman Inquisition, like its medieval predecessors, handed stubborn heretics over to the state to be burned, but the numbers involved were nothing like so large as those involved in the witch-trials – 72 Protestants burned for the whole of Italy in the second half of the sixteenth century, for example. The worst atrocities against Protestants were in fact often the work of Catholic secular governments rather than the Inquisition courts, like the burning of at least 273 men and women in England in a three-year period under Mary Tudor in the 1550s, a campaign in which the pace was set by the Crown and zealous local magistrates rather than by the Church, and in which the Inquisition was not involved at all.

By the late sixteenth century, indeed, the Roman Inquisition had largely turned its attention from the fight against heresy to the elimination of superstition and magic among the Catholic peasantry, and the use of the death penalty became extremely rare, except for moral offences like bestiality and buggery. Moreover, Inquisitorial proceedings, drastic and deadly as they might be, were mostly operated by conscientious churchmen who followed strict procedural rules, and who were interested in establishing inner motivation rather than mere external facts. As a result, a trial for heresy or witchcraft in front of an Inquisitor might be an altogether safer procedure for the accused than any comparable trial for the same crimes in secular courts. Famously, the Inquisitor Salazar y Frias conducted an exhaustive enquiry into accusations of witchcraft during the Basque witch panic of 1610, isolating dozens of suspects, taking them one by one to the scene of the alleged Sabbats, and carefully comparing their stories. He concluded that the whole thing was a fantasy, and earned himself the name 'the witches' advocate' in the process. This degree of care was probably unique in the history of the Inquisition, but it was absolutely inconceivable in any secular court before the modern era.

The Roman Inquisition survived the age of Enlightenment, to stagger on into the early nineteenth century, when it was swept away with much else of the *ancien régime* in the wake of the French Revolution. By that time it had become a byword for bigotry, intolerance and cruelty, and a number of classic Inquisition trials – the burning of the philosopher Giordano Bruno in Rome in 1600 and the silencing of Galileo – branded themselves into the imagination of secular and liberal Europe as the prime examples of the Church's hostility to liberty of thought, science, modernity.

That view of the Church was given some plausibility by the fact that the Congregation for the Inquisition, and of the Index, continued to exist even after their ability to invoke the aid of the secular police and the hangman had been abolished. Ecclesiastical delations for heresy continued to be secret, and the procedures for the censuring of theologians continued (and continue) to lack the openness, accountability and fairness to the accused we now expect of secular trials. The mentality of the Inquisition persisted. Above all, it persisted in the Church's continuing assumption that error had no rights, that it was the duty of Christian states to foster Catholic teaching, and to suppress whatever was alien to that teaching. The nineteenth- and early twentieth-century Church continued where it could to operate within the coercive framework established by Augustine fifteen centuries before. Religious freedom was thought – and taught – to be one of the poisoned fruits of the Enlightenment, an aspect of the human rebellion against revealed truth which we call sin. Protestants in a Catholic state (like Spain) might indeed hope for toleration, as a matter of pragmatism and *realpolitik*. But they could never expect freedom of religion and religious equality, for to concede that was to succumb to indifferentism, and to confirm the world in its errors.

All this was understandable enough, since many of the nineteenth-century states which prided themselves on maintaining freedom of religion, like the kingdom of Italy itself, in fact actively persecuted, harassed or robbed the Church. But the age-old insistence of the Church on the obligation of Christian states to enforce and promote the Catholic religion was overturned by the Second Vatican Council's 1965 Declaration on Religious Liberty, which taught clearly and unequivocally that freedom of religious thought and practice was not a matter of pragmatic concession in an imperfect political world, but a fundamental human right, and an aspect of our human dignity and freedom as the children of God.

The Council's teaching was, for many in the Church, a bombshell which cast radical doubt on the Church's teaching authority itself. How could 1,500 years of consistent Catholic teaching and practice on religious freedom be so radically mistaken? Was St Augustine, was St Thomas, were the popes who had established the Inquisition and the Index, who had promulgated Bulls permitting torture and the use of force in the service of gospel truth, were these all in error? These were not remote questions: in living memory the Vatican had approved arrangements by which the modern Spanish state had disadvantaged its Protestant citizens. These were the realities of the reigns of Pius XI and Pius XII, and not the far-off days of Innocent III and Gregory IX. To some, like Archbishop Lefebvre, all this was an abomination. It must be the Council which was in error, since in promulgating this new gospel of liberty it had broken with the constant teaching of a millennium and a half of Christian civilization. For Lefebvre and his supporters the question of religious freedom loomed at least as large in their disillusion with the Church of Vatican II as the loss of the Tridentine Mass.

As the third millennium approached, Pope John Paul II brooded on these things. He himself played a large part in the formulation and acceptance of the Council's declaration on religious liberty: the demand for freedom of conscience was a precious resource for him in his confrontation with Polish communism. He recognized the history of persecution as a blot on the Church's past, discrediting her in the eyes of the world, and hindering her task of proclaiming the Gospel of the dignity of redeemed humanity. He had already issued a statement accepting that the silencing of Galileo, though understandable in its own time, was an injustice. In his encyclical *Tertio Mellenio Adveniente*, he called on the Church to enter the new millennium 'with a clear awareness of all that has happened to her during the last ten centuries', and 'encouraging her children to purify themselves through repentance, of past errors and instances of infidelity, inconsistency and slowness to act': he singled out the history of religious persecution as a prime example of this moral and religious failure. As the year 2000 approached, the Jubilee themes of liberty to captives, the cancelling of debts, forgiveness and reconciliation, made the sorrowful acknowledgement of this woeful history of religious oppression seem appropriate and necessary.

At the end of October 1998, therefore, the Vatican's Jubilee commission summoned an historical symposium in the Vatican, to which the world's leading historians of the Inquisition were invited, in order to present a collective picture of the history and activities of the various Inquisitions from their first foundation to their dissolution in the nineteenth century. The object of this historical study (the results of which will soon be published in a massive scholarly collection devoted to the history of the Inquisition) was to provide the materials by which the Church might confront its own persecuting past, in a solemn act of 'purification of memory in penitence'. A specially constituted theological commission sat in on the historical sessions, and it was generally assumed that their task would be to prepare a theological reflection on the Inquisition for the pope, as the basis for an 'apology' like that published in 1997 on the Shoah.

Not everybody saw the sense of such an apology. In an eloquent and devastating intervention from the floor, the Jewish historian Carlo Ginsburg suggested that any talk of asking pardon for the past was unreal, an evasion of responsibility: the dead could not forgive, and he would rather hear the Church and the pope say simply that they were *ashamed* of the past, without asking easy absolution. There were in any case some uncomfortable ambivalences at the Symposium. For a start, the theologians appeared to be working fairly strictly to the brief set out by the pope in *Tertio Millenio Adveniente*. There, significantly, Pope John Paul spoke not of the need for the Church to repent its errors, but for the children of the Church to repent their sins and errors. There is more to this distinction than meets the eye: it seemed to many of us that Roman theology has simply not yet found a way of acknowledging that the institutional Church itself could err and sin. The main theological input to the Symposium, by the distinguished French theologian J. M. Garrigues, suggested that the Church's doctrinal *magisterium* had been 'silent' on the question of religious liberty until 1965, and that the 'political Augustinianism' by which persecution had been justified during the preceding millennium and a half, mistaken and repugnant to the gospel as it was, left the Church's doctrinal authority untouched.

Few of the historians present found this argument convincing, and there was some unease that any subsequent papal statement might attempt to reproduce the unreal distinction it seeks to make. The establishment, elaboration and privileging of the Inquisition by successive popes, the promulgation of Bulls against heresy and witchcraft, the creation of the Index of Prohibited Books, the shaping of the Church's fundamental relation to the states of medieval and modern Europe, and the uniform practice of repression and censorship at the heart of the Church's own central government – all this surely constitutes more than 'silence', and can hardly be treated as the incidental activity of some of the Church's children. Here the Church itself is implicated, and here too is something like that structural sin which the pope has discerned in the world's political and economic structures, operating within the heart of the Church herself.

I do not know whether the Pope was right to apologize for the Inquisition: there were those at the Symposium who thought that any such apology would ring hollow while the Congregation for the Doctrine of the Faith operates on its present terms of reference, and theologians can still be delated anonymously to Rome, and silenced without a proper hearing. However that may be, it is certain that we must confront and acknowledge in the sorry history of the Catholic Church's implication in religious violence, a collective and radical failure of vision and fidelity to the demands of the gospel, and not merely the individual sins and blindnesses of rather a lot of the Church's children.

19

Tradition and Authority

The Cardinal Hume Memorial Lecture,
Newcastle, 27 November 2003

My theme here is tradition and authority, and the tensions which may and sometimes do arise between them. The suggestion that there might be any such conflict or tension may strike you at first sight as a surprising one: it's more usual nowadays to see tradition and authority as twin sides of the same coin. You can try this out for yourself by getting on to the Internet and typing some such phrase as 'traditional Catholicism' into whatever search-engine you favour: you will come up with dozens of websites, from Mother Angelica to the Society of Saint Pius X, all of them more or less authoritarian in outlook, and all of them invoking tradition as essentially conservative, a way of confuting enemies and battening down the hatches against a wicked and innovating world.

As that suggests, the very concept of 'tradition' in contemporary Catholicism is highly contentious and politicized. The American Catholic writer and papal biographer George Weigel, for example, recently targeted what he called 'the culture of dissent' as one of the principal evils in today's Church, a culture which he believes has undermined truth and morality precisely by questioning Catholic tradition – by which he means the doctrinal teaching of the official Church, above all the pope. So among other things, Weigel calls for a purge of seminary staff who oppose or even hold 'a neutral stance towards the Church's tradition'. For him, that tradition is essentially a fixed body of teachings, like papal teaching on sexuality or the impossibility of ordaining women to the priesthood, demanding assent, though those teachings are often unpopular in the wider culture and even among Catholics seduced by the zeitgeist. This traditional teaching must therefore be 'learned', 'accepted' and 'defended'. 'Accepting' the tradition means a wholehearted willingness 'to think with the Church', a process conducted on the clear understanding that the rule of faith 'is determined by the Church's pastors, not by the Church's theologians' (George Weigel, *The Courage to be Catholic*, Perseus Books 2002, pp. 166–71).

The notion of 'thinking with the Church' is certainly funda-mental to any understanding of the meaning of the theological aspects of Catholic tradition. But tradition is here being envisaged essentially as a brake rather than an accelerator, a fixed body of unchanging information and prescription designed to limit and constrain dangerous freedom of thought. As is usual in such accounts, tradition is presented as in stark opposition to notions of conflict, debate and dissent. The notion that tradition is to be learned or learned from suggests that it is in some sense a school; but if so, in this conception the school is Dotheboys Hall, where the discipline is stern and the asking of questions is not allowed.

Of course, such an account of the meaning of tradition is not a neutral attempt at definition. Weigel's book was a response to the collapse of morale among American Catholics in the face of appalling but depressingly familiar revelations about clerical sexual misbehaviour, especially child abuse. American Catholics have been understandably traumatized by the transformation of the cosy clerical decencies of the Bells of St Mary's and the Bing Crosby era into the sordid world of Fr Paul Shanley, the Boston campaigner for the 'North American Man–Boy Love Associa-tion' (whose slogan is 'Eight is too late'), gaoled a few years ago for multiple cases of sexual molestation. According to Weigel, however, this is not essentially a sexual crisis, it is a crisis of fidelity. The real culprit is the 'culture of dissent' which has grown up since the Second Vatican Council and especially since 1968, when many priests and laypeople rejected the tradition in the shape of the teaching of *Humanae Vitae*. This all-pervasive

anti-traditionalist ethos, now maintained by an ageing, intellectually sterile but (happily) numerically shrinking 'cadre of
Catholic dissidents', gave birth to what he calls 'Catholic Lite',
a vacuous sub-Catholicism which apes the moral and intellectual bankruptcy of liberal Protestantism, reducing the true
Church to a mere denomination. American seminaries in the
late 1960s and 1970s replaced genuine theological formation
with 'pop' psychology, and abandoned any attempt to inculcate
Catholic orthodoxy and Catholic morality, above all Catholic
teaching on chastity. The result was a slide into moral squalor.
Gay clerical students danced with one another at seminary
parties, no one was asked what (if anything) they believed, no
one was taught to pray or live a priestly lifestyle. Priestly
vocation was eroded by an unfocused emphasis on lay
ministries. The fiasco was worsened by the inadequacies of the
American episcopate, who, seduced by managerial and
consensual models of leadership, and terrified of appearing
politically incorrect, abandoned theology and dismally failed to
offer any real Christian direction to priests or laity.

Weigel's book is very explicitly directed at the current ills of
the American Catholic Church: and, since he is a well-informed
and intelligent man, he hits real targets in the course of his
analysis. But his book belongs to a familiar enough type of conservative jeremiad, and I have lingered over his account of
tradition here not because I think it is specially penetrating, but
because it is certainly representative, exposing apprehensions
widely shared outside the specifics of the American scene, and
with significant backing nowadays in Rome. In particular, I am
worried by the authoritarian character of Weigel's proposed
remedy for the present malaise of the Church – the creation of
what he calls 'a harder, more brilliant form of Catholicism', in
which the still sadly influential 'Lite Brigade' will be marginalized and replaced by 'self-consciously orthodox Catholics', men
'known to be defenders of the Church and of the Pontificate'.
This means the appointment to the episcopate of priests in their
thirties and forties, formed 'in the image of John Paul II'. These
new priests and their teachers will be 'unimpeachably

orthodox', and that is why there must be a systematic purge of seminaries, applying doctrinal tests to ensure they are staffed only by ardent defenders of 'the most bitterly contested teachings of the Catholic Church': in those seminaries, future priests must be trained to accept the whole of the Catholic tradition without criticizing it.

A moment's reflection on how traditions actually function in the real world will suggest why all this is deeply misleading. All living traditions need and are nourished by some degree of self-scrutiny and debate, and they are not undermined by it: indeed, where they become fixed and immune from such self-scrutiny, they die. Tradition is not a weight holding us down, but a tool for fresh discovery. This is as true for religious traditions as for any other kind.

For in any case, traditions are usually as much about acquiring skills as accumulating propositions – information. A straightforward example of a highly traditional pursuit is learning to be a musician – let's say a violinist. When you first begin to learn the violin, you do indeed have to learn the essentials of musical theory: how to hold your bow, how to position your fingers to play the right chords, all of this fairly mechanical and parrot fashion. There is not much music-making in any of this, just mastering the basics. As you improve, you are likely to begin to imitate musicians you admire – your violin teacher or Yehudi Menuhin or Nigel Kennedy – and that sort of imitation is an essential aspect of mastering the instrument for yourself. Finally, with real mastery, comes the ability to use the traditional skills and knowledge you have laboriously acquired to contribute something distinctively your own: you may come to criticize and reject the techniques and musical choices of your former models, and if you are a really great player or composer, you may inaugurate radical changes of technique or musical understanding – you add to the tradition, leaving it different from the way you found it.

The formation and transmission of the Church's tradition is of course a good deal more complex and multi-faceted than learning to play the violin: my point is not that this comparison tells us everything we need to know about what Catholic tradition is and how it works, but merely to draw attention to the fact that accounts of that tradition which edit out or deny the necessary presence of conflict, debate, invention and innovation, don't do justice to what is in fact a fundamental feature of all traditions whatever.

This denial of debate and plurality of voices within every vital tradition, tradition understood as obedience to authority, is of course not new. It was very much a feature of nineteenth-century Ultramontanism. Famously, during the debates over papal infallibility in 1870 at the first Vatican Council, the Dominican Archbishop of Bologna, Cardinal Guidi, dared to suggest that the pope could not make an infallible utterance without first consulting with the other bishops, who functioned as witnesses to the tradition of their various churches. In a scarifying private audience, the pope, Pius IX, berated him as a traitor. What need was there for other bishops as 'witnesses of the tradition', he demanded: 'I *am* the tradition.'

Pio Nono's collapse of the plurality and choric character of tradition – many different voices making up a harmony, not a monotone – into the single voice of the pope, serves to expose simultaneously both the attraction and the historical poverty of all such attempts to short-circuit the mess, complexity and simple difficulty of discerning truth in our shared human experience. Agreement in the great Councils of the Church was not the product of blinding flashes of revelation or the tranquil reiteration of familiar and uncontentious unanimities, or rubber-stamping the declarations of popes: the Church's foundation doctrines emerged – and emerge – by debate, conflict, convergence, and eventually consensus: painful and costly processes which may take decades and even centuries to crystallize. The nineteenth-century Ultramontanes, like their twenty-first-century descendants, yearned for history without bewilderment or tears, and looked to the tradition, and the *magisterium* as the mouthpiece of tradition, for a living oracle which could short-circuit human confusion and limitation: it was and is the attempt to confront the uncertainties of our age with instant assurance, revelation on tap. But what such a project amounts to, in fact, is the effective abolition of tradition, abandoning attention to the complex and not always harmonious chorus of our shared past, and replacing it with the monotone voice of present authority.

The reality of the Church's tradition seems to me quite different, much more like an ancient and complex building than a neatly tabulated set of questions and answers. I am fond of the analogy between tradition and one building in particular, the church of San Clemente in Rome: an ancient church near the Colosseum, which has been in the care of the Irish Dominicans since the seventeenth century. It has a magnificently carved and gilded ceiling, inserted by an eighteenth-century pope, and a glorious medieval pavement, all swirling circles of porphyry and gold. Behind the canopied altar, frescoed apostles surround an austere Christ in majesty. But the glory of the apse is its glittering twelfth-century mosaic, a crucifixion in which Christ is surrounded on the cross by doves, while the cross itself rises from a luxuriant blue and green tree of life. From it flow streams of water, from which thirsty deer drink. In its shelter, animals and birds feed and play, the weapons of war lie discarded, and human life goes on – a woman throws corn to her chickens, a shepherd tends his sheep.

The San Clemente mosaic is a theology in itself. But it is only the start of what the building has to offer. For centuries everyone thought that what you can see of the church above ground was all there is. But nineteenth-century repairs uncovered behind the plaster a baffling set of arches placed at floor level. The friars dug, and discovered under their feet another complete basilica, dating from the sixth century and, deeper still, a first-century Roman street, a wealthy house which was thought to be the house of St Clement, one of the earliest popes, and a complete Mithraic temple. In the buried basilica was a set of early medieval frescoes of the legend of St Clement, depicting the recovery of his relics from the Crimea and their reburial in the church in the ninth century, and the grave of St Cyril apostle of the Slavs. And recently, excavations connected with some building repairs have uncovered yet another amazing aspect of the site, a hitherto unknown complex of buildings which includes an intact sixth-century baptistery, complete with marble pool and bishop's chair.

The whole history of the Church is encapsulated in San Clemente, and the building carries the marks of sin as well as of glory. The frescoes of St Clement and the grave of St Cyril date from an age when the popes were engaged in bitter conflict with the patriarchs of Constantinople for control of the church in the Balkans. That struggle ended in the schism between the Eastern and Western churches. And the present basilica of San Clemente was built because the old church had been burned to the ground by Norman bandits, summoned to Rome to 'rescue' the reforming but overbearing pope Gregory VII from the German king Henry IV, who had seized the city and appointed an anti-pope.

For me, San Clemente is a near-perfect expression of Catholic tradition, layer upon layer of shared prayer, thought, sufferings – and sin. Like the mosaic, the church yields its meaning only to slow meditation and close attention to the traces of the past which it contains, some of it half-buried and forgotten, and, as in the recent excavations, it is always being rediscovered, but only with labour and cost and love, and a certain amount of luck. It is able to surprise and shock us, as well as confirm in us what we already knew; it is able to make us stop in our tracks and think again, and able always to make us catch our breath with its sheer majesty and beauty.

We grow from our own past, and we only flourish when we are in touch with that past. But you can't be in touch with all of your past all of the time, and you emphatically can't put people in touch with their past by telling them to shut up and listen to the boss. Our tradition is not a dossier of teachings to be learned by heart and ticked off one by one. It's an ancient house, filled with rooms we have forgotten, full of wisdom and beauty, but full too of the scars of old mistakes. Faithfulness to that tradition is not a matter of uncritical obedience to authority; it is a shared labour of learning, in which we work together to draw new and surprising growth from the old soil. Like the friars of San Clemente, we have to go on digging.

As a monk, I think that Cardinal Hume would have warmed to this understanding of tradition as the trace of a complex shared life, rather than as a clear-cut compendium of answers. Monastic life itself offers a similar model of the complex and sometimes contradictory character of the tradition, with its immersion in a rule which is both a distillation of humane common sense and of divine revelation as to what human community should be like, and with its lived-out conviction that wisdom and truth are difficult, and don't come quickly, but from shared and life-long labour, from the *lectio divina* – sustained, prayerful and patient attention to inherited resources and realities which we may have no immediate sympathy or use for, an attention given not out of antiquarian interest, or to keep people in military step, but as resources for living.

Of course it's not very original to see monastic life in this way, as the epitome of what it means to live within a tradition, and as a model of just what it is that the Church has to offer the world. One of my favourite books is Walter Miller's science-fiction novel *A Canticle for Leibowitz*, a story about the rebuilding of world civilization after a new dark ages brought on by nuclear war. In the aftermath of that war the world had turned its back on technology and science, and most of the scientists had been lynched. The novel focuses on a fictional religious order, the Order of St Leibowitz, dedicated to the preservation and copying of the remnants of the world's learning: monks in the great desert fortress monastery (somewhere in Arizona I would guess) copy and illuminate elaborate symbolic diagrams which, as we realize but they do not, are in fact electrical circuit charts and machine blueprints. As the world had collapsed in nuclear ruins, the Church survived, though Rome was liquidated and the papacy is now established somewhere in America. The monks preserve civilization in a world populated by cannibalistic desert mutants and ruled by robber barons. In due course there is a new

Renaissance, and a new scientific revolution, in which the monastery's precious archive plays its part. But once more pride and sin precipitate war: as the novel closes, the monks of St Leibowitz set off for the stars in a spaceship, aboard which are a group of cardinals, among them the next pope: behind them, nuclear winter descends.

Miller's book is a witty meditation on the difference between knowledge and wisdom, and on the relation of the Church and its tradition to human culture, in an essentially Augustinian framework. Everything in the novel changes, except the desperate sinfulness of the human heart, and the ancient abiding certainties of the Church and her liturgy: at the end of the fictional fourth millennium that liturgy is still in Latin and the forms of the Christian life are exactly as they had been in 1959, down to the gloves and buskins worn by the bishops for High Mass. Miller's grand vision of the collapse and flux of human society through millennia betrays not the slightest premonition of the revolution which, in 1959, the year of the novel's publication, was about to transform the Church, which for Miller was the one constant in a world perpetually falling apart.

Miller was by no means alone in seeing in the externals of pre-Conciliar Catholicism as having an immemorial air about them. Many Catholics, perhaps most of us then, saw in the Church's rituals and symbols timeless realities which had never and could never change. The work of the Irish poet Seamus Heaney resonates with me in this respect, for we shared similar childhoods. His writing is saturated with testimony to the fascination and symbolic power of the external manifestations of Catholic tradition as they were in the 1950s: he has more than once commented on the influence on him of what he calls 'the gorgeous and inane phraseology of the Catechism' and of the titles of Mary in the Litany of Loretto – Tower of Gold, Ark of the Covenant, Gate of Heaven, Morning Star, Health of the Sick, Refuge of Sinners 'Bedding the ear with a kind of linguistic hard-core that could be built on some day' (*Preoccupations*, p. 45).

The visual and verbal minutiae of pre-Conciliar Catholicism

are everywhere in Heaney's writing, with a cinematic focus which is a testimony to their imaginative power as well as to his eloquence – the watered-silk coloured markers on the big altar book, the striped and damasked black chasuble used for funerals, the sense of 'splitting the gold-bar thickness' of the pages of a missal, the 'thin fastidious movement, up and out and in' of the priest handing his biretta to the server, the 'unexpectedly secular' appearance of a priest's boots under his lace-edged alb. Such images constantly surface, often in extraordinary places, not least the bedroom: who else, I wonder, has evoked the touch of a wife's body, sexily wet and cold from the bath, like this:

> first coldness of the underbreast
> like a ciborium in the palm

or compared the teasing openings of a silk nightdress to:

> the little fitted deep-slit drapes,
> on and off the holy vessels.

Imaginative resonance, of course, is not enough: powerful and permanent as the impact of these external details from the tradition have been on Heaney's imagination, for him the spell has somehow been broken, the god has departed. That glimpse of an altar missal with its coloured ribbon page-markers comes from a poem which reflects explicitly on the once apparent timelessness and super-reality of a world of traditional symbols which has now slipped away; its title is 'In Illo Tempore':

> The big missal splayed
> and dangled silky ribbons
> of emerald and purple and watery white.
> Intransitively we would assist,
> confess, receive. The verbs
> assumed us. We adored.
> And we lifted our eyes to the nouns.

Altar-stone was dawn and monstrance noon,
The word rubric itself a blood-shot sunset.

Now I live by a famous strand
where seabirds cry in the small hours
like incredible souls
and even the wall of the promenade
that I press down on for conviction
hardly tempts me to credit it.

This is about more than religion, of course: the symbolic density of Heaney's inherited Catholicism is here treated as a metaphor for a world we have all lost, some prelapsarian state of linguistic and imaginative naivete, a creaturely bliss innocent of the slippage and elusiveness of meaning, from which the sophisticated poet and we, his readers and contemporaries, have been cast out. Whether or not we share the loss of religious faith which the poem implies in the fading of the power of its visible markers, that loss has itself become a metaphor for an all-embracing erosion of meaning and certainty, the plight of modernity which none of us altogether escapes.

Heaney's poems are written from the other side of a divide which, for the Catholic Church, was about to open in the very year in which Miller's novel first appeared. *A Canticle for Leibowitz* was published in 1959, less than twelve months after the death of Pope Pius XII, himself something of an apparently timeless icon of how the ideal pope should behave and even what he should look like. Soon after his accession, his successor, John XXIII, announced his intention to convene the Second Vatican Council. That Council would dramatically change Catholic perceptions of the nature and force of tradition by harnessing the resources of the remote past liturgically and theologically, not as instruments of conservation but of change: the Council would sweep away precisely those external markers of what was often in fact relatively recent tradition, which to Miller had seemed such fixed and timeless components of what the Church stood for. And although much of the theological impetus for these changes came from a generation of theologians like Yves Congar and Henri de Lubac, whose work was based on profound reflection on the tradition and its meaning, in the ferment after the Council the very notion of 'tradition' itself became suspect to many. Some of the practical reforms of the late 1960s and 1970s emanated not from the renewal of Catholic theology and worship in the light of a larger and deeper exploration of the whole of tradition which the Council called for and initiated, but from a well-intentioned liberalism which confused renewal with modernity, Christian hope with secular optimism, and progress with the abandonment of contact with a past imagined as defunct and deadening. Some of the practical work of reform, in liturgy and in discipline was carried out hastily, insensitively and without real understanding of or sympathy for what was constitutive of rather than optional in the catholic past. It became abundantly clear that tradition and traditional practices had been felt by many to be not a resource but a suffocating burden.

This was by no means all or mainly the fault of those who called for change at any price. There was plenty going on then to give 'tradition' a bad name, for many of those who repudiated both the spirit and the actual teachings of the Council, like the followers of Archbishop Levebvre, now arrogated to themselves the name 'Traditionalist', and appealed against the Council to precisely such a repressive and rigid understanding of tradition, as if that tradition were a body of positive law forbidding growth, rather than a living and liberating testimony to the multiple and unending transformations of Catholicism in its journey through times and cultures. And too often that frozen and oppressive understanding of tradition has been accepted – and in consequence dismissed – by Catholics at large. Hence the philistine scramble away from so much that was precious in our liturgical, devotional and theological inheritance, in the name of renewal.

I want to turn now to what I consider to be one of the saddest and most serious casualties of this wholesale departure from a tradition seen simply as the dead hand of the past. This was the effective abolition of one of the defining aspects of pre-Conciliar Catholicism, fasting and abstinence. Whether one sees the impact of the Council as a blessing or as a blight, here is a change which unmistakably represented a radical discontinuity within Catholic tradition, a decisive break with the past. The ritual observance of dietary rules – fasting and abstinence from meat in Lent, and abstinence from meat and meat products every Friday, as well as the Eucharistic fast from midnight before the reception of Communion – were as much defining marks of Catholicism before the Council, as abstention from pork is a defining characteristic of Judaism. The Friday abstinence in particular was a focus of Catholic identity which transcended class and educational barriers, and which united 'good' and 'bad' Catholics in a single eloquent observance. Here was a universally recognized expression of Catholicism which was nothing to do with priests or authority. But instead of seeing this as one of its greatest strengths, it was often used as an argument against Friday abstinence that bad or badly instructed Catholics, like those often dismissed as the 'Bog Irish', men who it was thought drank their wages or beat their wives, yet who were nevertheless punctilious in eating fish on Fridays – they were keeping the mere externals, it was claimed, while ignoring the essence of 'real' Christianity. What was needed was a more spiritual sort of religion, which offered no such crutches to lame practice.

And that was the view which won out. Fasting is now confined to a derisory two days of the year, and compulsory Friday abstinence has been replaced by a genteel and totally individualistic injunction to do some penitential act on a Friday – an injunction, incidentally, which most Catholics know nothing about. What had been a corporate mark of identity has been marginalized into an individualistic option.

Why did it happen? Certainly not because fasting was in some sense peripheral to Catholicism, an inessential and minor aspect of our tradition which needed tidying away. We touch here one of the universals of the world's great religions. Fasting was an important element in Israelite religion, and Christ's own defence of his disciples' failure to fast during his lifetime specifically envisaged that they would fast after his death. From at least the end of the first century, Christians have observed Fridays, and later the forty days of Lent, as fast days in commemoration of the passion. At the heart of Catholicism for a millennium and a half lay a dialectical dividing of time, a rhythmic movement between the poles of fast and feast, Lent and Easter, renunciation and affirmation

Catholics shared that rhythm with most of the world's great religious traditions, of course, a fact which ought to have suggested that there was something essential about it not only for our specific identities as Catholic Christians, but as religious beings – as human. But since 1967 it has effectively been abandoned, or turned into a private, individualistic and therefore invisible devotional option. What was once a truly corporate observance, reminding us of the passion of Christ, of our own spiritual poverty, and even more concretely, of the material poverty of most of the human race, reminding us what it was like to be hungry, has become another individual consumer choice, like going on a diet. Though we pay liturgical lip-service to the old dialectic, and still nominally keep Lent, in practice all our time now has become 'ordinary time'.

It would be easy to show the folly of all this simply from the point of view of social anthropology, as Professor Mary Douglass did brilliantly in her book *Natural Symbols*. Religious communities depend on the differentiation provided by such shared observances to sustain their identities – we need only look at the Jews to see how powerful dietary regulations can be as an enduring focus of such identity. The long and noble pilgrimage of Israel through a multitude of cultures and times, without a temple, without a priesthood, has been possible, at least in part, because of the unifying and sustaining effect of their dietary laws. The Jews knew who they were because of what they did and did not eat.

Christian fasting and abstinence did not of course spring from a ritual distinction between clean and unclean meats, but it was just as deeply imbedded in theological conviction as the older dispensation. Its abandonment was not therefore a simple

change in devotional habit, but the signal of a radical discontinuity in the tradition, and a decisive shift in theological
perception.

There was another issue here. The theological and practical
shift represented by this abandonment of an ancient part of the
tradition was not merely a matter of theological emphasis, and
more too than a question of whether ascetical exercises like
fasting are good for the character. What was also at stake was the
Church's prophetic integrity, its claim to solidarity with the
poor. Considered from this perspective, compulsory fasting and
abstinence, practised regularly, routinely and in common, was a
recognition by the Church that identification with the poor and
hungry, with those who know themselves to be needy before
God because they were needy among men, is not an option for
Catholics, but a necessary and definitive sign of our redemption,
as essential in its way as attendance at Mass. The Church has
always linked personal asceticism and the search for holiness
with this demand for mercy and justice to the poor – the Lenten
trilogy of prayer, fasting and almsgiving is fundamental,
structural. In abandoning real and regular fasting and abstinence
as a corporate and normative expression of our faith – by
making it optional – the Church forfeited one of its most
eloquent prophetic signs. There is a world of difference
between a private devotional gesture, the action of the specially
pious, and the prophetic witness of the whole community, the
matter-of-fact witness, repeated week by week, that to be
Christian is to stand among the needy.

What was striking about the instructions on all this issued by
the English bishops in abolishing compulsory Friday abstinence
in 1967 was the total absence of any attempt to explain
the power and meaning of the traditional observances. The
American bishops did much better: while also making the
matter optional, they offered a powerful and sympathetic
discussion of the religious reasons for the old observance, and
urged American Catholics to continue the practice as a gesture
of solidarity with and gratitude for the passion of Christ, as an
act of fidelity to the Christian past, and to help 'preserve a saving

and necessary difference from the spirit of the world'. In total contrast, the English bishops recited the problems and inconveniences surrounding abstinence: many people, they pointed out, have their main meal at work, in a canteen; social events are often arranged for Fridays. In all this, abstinence made Catholics an awkward squad. As the bishops wrote:

> While an alternative dish is often available, it is questioned whether it is advisable in our mixed society for a Catholic to appear singular in this matter. Non-Catholics know and accept that we do not eat meat on Fridays, but often they do not understand why we do not, and in consequence regard us as odd! *ol — we ma it Never seem odd!*

Fasting was rote piety, it encouraged superficiality or hypocrisy, it inconvenienced one's neighbours, it made us seem odd at school, at work, at meals in other people's houses.

All this of course was precisely to miss the point, for the whole rationale of symbolic gestures requires that they *do* disrupt and disturb the secular order. Their power to witness not only to others but to ourselves comes precisely from their awkwardness. Abolish such observances and you strike at the heart of tradition, you abolish the distinctive language of belief, and you do it at your peril. Catholic value cannot be sustained without its proper symbolic expression. You can't know your spiritual need unless you express it in physical need. We can know the fundamental neediness which is the foundation of faith, only if we feel our involvement with those who must fast because they have nothing to eat.

But none of those arguments prevailed, or were even explored. The bishops saw in the plight of the hungry not a reason for communal fasting as a gesture of solidarity and a call to justice and charity, but as a demonstration of the emptiness of any such gesture. Many Catholics, they wrote,

> have begun to ask themselves if going without meat on Friday is penance enough. Some find it no penance at all.

Meanwhile in Asia, Africa and South America many
Catholics have to go without meat not only on Fridays but
every day. Millions are starving or at least underfed. The
Bishops have therefore decided that the best way of
carrying out our Lord's command to do penance is for
each of us to choose our own way of self-denial every
Friday.

As Mary Douglass commented scornfully, 'Thus was the old
ritual abolished . . . Now there is no cause for others to regard
us as odd. Friday no longer rings the great cosmic symbols of
expiation and atonement: it is not symbolic at all . . . Now the
English Catholics are like everyone else' (*Natural Symbols*, 1996,
Routledge, pp. 43–5, from which my quotations from the
American and English bishops' documents have been taken).

   The abandonment of fasting and abstinence was symptomatic
of a more widespread drift, the levelling down and disappearance of much that was distinctive in the symbolic lives of
Catholics, the network of observances and prayers which
shaped and sustained our lives as Catholics. That drift continues.
Holy days of obligation are celebrated on the nearest Sunday so
as to avoid inconvenience or the interruption of secular patterns
of living, Sunday Mass can be heard on a Saturday to make way
for a day's work or cleaning the car or a morning in bed with
the papers, like our pagan neighbours: from time to time there
is talk of a fixed date for Easter and Whitsun – all part of the
minimizing of symbolic distinctiveness, in the service of secular
convenience, and a slow form of ritual suicide for any religious
tradition.

   For this aspect of tradition, the dimension of symbolic distinctiveness preserved in the ancient patterns of the worship and
ritual life of the Church, seems to me at least as central to
Catholic identity as many of the doctrinal positions worried
about by those who conceive of tradition primarily as a body
of authoritative teaching. In fact, I believe that the massive
desensitization to the meaning and value of symbolic gesture
and symbolic differentiation which we have witnessed in the

two generations since the Council, and which underlay
calamities like the jettisoning of fasting and abstinence, would
not have been possible if we had not long since parked responsibility for all that with someone else – an abstraction called the
magisterium – thereby absolving ourselves from understanding
and teaching the independent value of our symbols and traditional practices. How else could the Catholic people have
allowed their pastors to assail and abolish these ancient continuities in the name of mere convenience and the avoidance of
oddity? The authoritarian narrowing of the tradition to, in
essence, a body of doctrines to be believed and orders from
above to be obeyed, was a decisive factor in desensitizing
ordinary Catholics, clerical as well as lay, to the beauty and
independent value of their inherited observances, matters over
which no authority has or ought to have absolute control. The
ordinary members of the Orthodox and Byzantine Rite
Catholic churches have a far less authoritarian mentality than
ours, a far more widespread and lively sense of the richness of
their traditions of prayer and practice, a far more secure sense of
ownership by the people of the symbols which provide
continuity with the Christian past, and which shape and enable
a Christian response to the challenges of the present.

There has been a conscious element of paradox or at any rate
of dialectic in what I have had to say about tradition in this
essay. On the one hand, it seems to me that authoritarian
attempts to identify Catholic tradition with a narrow and ideologically driven agenda of doctrinal positions are to be resisted.
At one level, obviously enough, Catholic tradition is a very
simple and unmysterious thing: a mother teaching her child to
make the sign of the cross is communicating both the heart and,
in the end, the whole of what Christianity has to say. At another
level, tradition is an immense and almost infinitely various
treasure house of Christian experience, the trace of the gospel as
it has been articulated and lived out over millennia, in societies
and times almost unimaginably different and distant from us and
from each other: there is no single voice of the tradition. That
treasurehouse is not in the least tidy, because it reflects all the

variety and contradiction of human hearts and human minds responding to and searching for their God. It is the treasure house of the scribe, from which we can hope to bring forth things old and new, things which challenge and surprise as well as things which confirm and encourage. We should let nobody tell us that they know all that it contains, or try to prescribe or constrain in advance what it has to tell us. We need open minds and open hearts when we wrestle with the past and ask questions of it, and the answers it will provide are in nobody's pocket, not even the pope's.

But equally, we can only experience the tradition as a source of freedom, and as a resource for the future rather than the dead weight of the past, if we live close to it, and are willing to submit ourselves to its disciplines. In the euphoria and the confusions after the Council, tradition in the sense which I have been exploring was too often seen as useless lumber, a drag on modernity, ritual irrelevance hindering an open and loving response to the needs of the world. We were too inclined to forget that a Catholic response to the needs of the world needs to be Catholic as well as responsive, if it is to be of any use to a world that has never needed the wisdom of Catholicism more.

The realization that perhaps too much was carelessly abandoned in the years after the Council is now widespread, indeed has become something of an official view in the later years of the pontificate of John Paul II, and it has helped fuel sometimes scary projects for a restoration of 'real Catholicism', programmes in which the vigorous exercise of authority from above loom very large. I am suspicious of all such programmes, for they seem to me as bad as the ills they seek to remedy. There are no quick fixes: tradition cannot be rebuilt to a neat programme and by orders from Rome. What our shared past has to tell us can only be excavated by shared endeavour, by a painful and constant process of re-education and rediscovery: in that process, we start from where we are, not where we wish we had stayed. We cannot afford the pleasures and false securities of reaction. But that isn't to say that in our march into the needs and opportunities of the twenty-first century we should not try once more to summon up some of the deeper resources of our own tradition, and try to rediscover within it once more some of the supports which helped our fathers and mothers to live the Gospel. We could do worse than start by rededicating ourselves to the shared observance of fasting and abstinence.

[Handwritten marginal notes, partially legible:]

I have used likely Dunstan in looking at feasts as fasts :- Methodism much of that scattered

much earlier than :- Catholicism. I can't get worked up about fish as fasting! Yet we Must explore our tradition (eg Charles Wesley's hymns) before they scatter. Are our & their Methodism left flew!

Perhaps the victory meaning comes from would be a habitat equivalent — the 'CEM'

— The book is a fascinating exploration by English Catholicism (leading historian)